W9-AUM-401

Bicycle Repair

Step by Step

The Full-Color Manual of Bicycle Maintenance and Repair

Rob van der Plas

*Illustrated
by the author*

Bicycle Books – San Francisco

© Robert van der Plas, 1994

First edition 1994-X

Published by:
Bicycle Books, Inc.
P.O. Box 2038
Mill Valley, CA 94942
U.S.A.

Distributed to the book trade by:
U.S.A.:   National Book Network, Lanham, MD
Canada: Raincoast Book Distributing, Vancouver, BC

Cover design:
Kent Lytle, Lytle Design, Alameda, CA

Photography:
Neil van der Plas, Nic Jones, and Rob van der Plas
Frontispiece photograph taken at *American Cyclery*, San Francisco.
Bicycles for the photographs courtesy *A Bicycle Odyssey*, Sausalito, *Mill Valley Cyclery*, Mill Valley, *Mountain Avenue*, San Francisco, *Fahrradgesellschaft*, Germany, and *Gazelle*, Holland.
Some other components made available by *Shimano Europe* and *Sachs*.

Printed in Hong Kong

Cataloging in Publication Data:
Van der Plas, Robert, 1938–
Bicycle Repair: Step by Step, The Full-Color Manual of Bicycle Maintenance and Repair. Bibliography: p. Includes index.
1. Bicycles and Bicycling—manuals, handbooks, etc.
2. Authorship.
I. Title.

Library of Congress Catalog Card No. 93-72508

ISBN 0-933201-58-3

About the Author

Rob van der Plas is a professional engineer and a lifelong cyclist who has written about the subject for specialized magazines since 1975. His *Penguin Bicycle Handbook*, first published in 1981, has long been a classic amongst general bicycle books in Great Britain.

In 1984, when the modern mountain bike was still in its infancy, his *Mountain Bike Book*, the first book on the subject, was published. Since then, several other books by him were published by Springfield Books in the U.K., Bicycle Books in the U.S., and various Dutch and German publishing houses. They include *The Bicycle Repair Book*, *The Bicycle Touring Manual*, *The Bicycle Racing Guide*, *Bicycle Technology*, *Mountain Bike Maintenance*, *The Mountain Bike Book*, and *Roadside Bicycle Repair*.

Author's Preface

For this book, I owe thanks to many people who helped make it better than I could have done myself. Special thanks to Tony Tom of A Bicycle Odyssey for lending me bikes and other equipment to be photographed, to Gene of American Cyclery for letting me photograph his shop for the frontispiece photo. I would also like to thank July Harrell for weeding out the British bias in my bicycle terminology and her help with the photos, and Michele Jones for her editing and proofreading. Finally, my special thanks to Nic Jones and my son Neil for their patience in doing most of the photography.

Within the narrowly defined scope of a repair manual, I have made every effort to include here all the information that seems relevant. I have purposely included not only the latest and currently fashionable equipment, but also older and less common components, in the hope of making the book as useful as possible to as many people as possible. If you, the cyclist, know of better ways to tackle certain jobs, or would like to see specific other maintenance and repair procedures included, I would appreciate hearing from you.

Send any comments you may have to the author, care of the publisher (see copyright page for the postal address). Your suggestions for improved repair techniques may be incorporated in subsequent editions of the book.

TABLE OF CONTENTS

CHAPTER 1

Know Your Bicycle

Above: Modern road bike with drop handlebars, narrow tires, and 16-speed derailleur gearing.

Below: Mountain bike with flat handlebars, wide tires, and 21-speed gearing. The model shown is equipped with above-the-bar shifters and front "shocks."

THE present book is intended to help you keep your bicycle in optimal condition. It gives you essentially all the information you will ever need to keep the bike in optimal condition, and to enable you to fix it when it does malfunction.

The approach of the book is simple: define the problem, identify the cause, and show what to do about it. I will go about it as systematically as possible, first explaining what can be the cause of a specific problem, then proceeding with a list of required tools—or ways to substitute for the right tools, if they can't be rounded up—and finally applying step-by-step instructions for alleviating the problem. Photographic illustrations and the occasional detail drawing allow you to identify parts and tools at a glance.

The emphasis is on the type of bicycles mostly sold these days, regular derailleur bikes and mountain bikes. However, this book also explains in detail the equipment that is only found on other models, such as folding bikes, roadsters or even carrier bicycles. Thus, the 3-speed hub, drum and roller-lever brakes, and even generator lighting equipment are covered by adequate instructions for their maintenance.

The Parts of the Bicycle

To do any work on the bike, it is necessary first to know just what we are talking about and what the various components of the machine are called. I shall now briefly describe its major components. Components will be treated separately as units, and together as groups. The following functional groups may be distinguished:

☐ The gearing system   ☐ The steering system
☐ The brakes   ☐ The frame
☐ The drivetrain   ☐ The saddle
☐ The wheels   ☐ Accessories

The Gearing System

Nowadays, this usually means derailleur gearing, although hub-gears are still used on some bikes. Chapter 4 gives the details. A derailleur system is made up of the front and rear derailleurs, which move the chain from one combination of chainring and sprocket to another, and the shift levers mounted on the handlebars or the frame's downtube (depending on the kind of bike), as well as flexible cables that connect each shifter with its derailleur. On some simple bikes, a 3-, 5-, or 7-speed hub is used instead of the derailleurs and

Above: Drivetrain on a bicycle with derailleur gearing, showing an 8-speed cassette in the back and 2 chainrings in the front.

is operated by means of a shifter on the handlebars, while the traditional American utility bike and the cruiser often have no gears.

The Brakes

The brakes are also (usually) controlled by means of flexible cables from levers mounted on the handlebars. Once you pull the brake lever, the brake itself stops the wheel by squeezing two brake pads against the sides of the wheel rim. The various types of brakes used on the mountain bike will be covered in Chapter 5.

The Drivetrain

The drivetrain comprises the parts that transmit the rider's propulsive force or torque to the rear wheel. As described in Chapter 6, it consists of the crankset, the pedals, the chain, the chainrings, and the freewheel on the rear wheel hub.

The Wheels

The wheels, covered in Chapter 7, have flexible inner tubes and separate tires, except for true racing bikes, which have sewn-up tubular tires, or "sew-ups." The tires are mounted on an aluminum rim that is held to the hub by means of spokes hooked into the hub flanges and screwed into nipples at the rim. The hub is held to the frame or the fork either with nuts threaded onto the axle or with a quick-release mechanism.

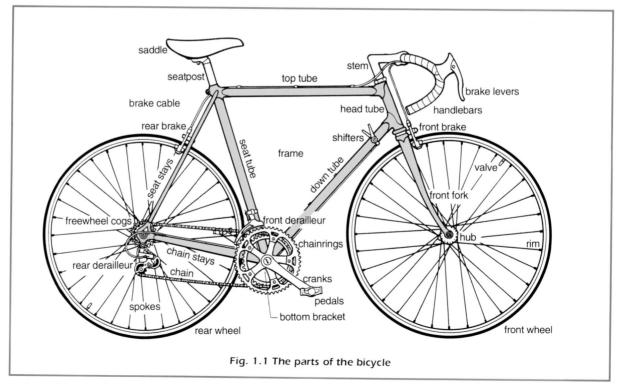

Fig. 1.1 The parts of the bicycle

Above: Wheel removal is made easy with quick-release hubs. Once the QR lever is flipped into the "open" position, the wheel can be slipped in or out.

Below: To remove or install a rear wheel, hold back the derailleur so the chain clears the sprocket cluster.

The Steering System

The steering system, which is analyzed in Chapter 8, comprises the parts that allow balancing and steering the bike. These include the front fork, handlebars, stem, and headset bearings. This group allows the steering system to pivot relative to the rest of the bike when the handlebars are turned.

The Frame

The frame is covered in Chapter 9. It forms the backbone of the bicycle, on which the other components are installed. The frame comprises tubes that have been welded or bonded together. They are the main frame (head tube, top tube, down tube and seat tube), as well as the pairs of thinner tubes that make up the rear triangle (seat stays and chain stays). In addition, there is a bottom bracket, at the point where down tube, seat tube and chain stays meet, and drop-outs which accept the rear axle. Fortunately, the frame rarely needs repair work.

The Saddle

The saddle is mounted to a tubular seatpost, which in turn is clamped into the frame's seat tube. Its height and angle can be adjusted by means of the clamping devices that hold the seatpost to the frame and the saddle to the seatpost, respectively. This subject is described in Chapter 10.

Accessories

Accessories are additional components that can be installed on the bicycle. The maintenance and/or installation of the saddle adjuster (Hite-Rite), lighting equipment, luggage racks, fenders and chainring guard are covered in Chapter 11.

Quick Fix-Its

In this section, you will find brief descriptions of the most frequently occurring minor maintenance operations that you will encounter: the use of the quick-release for wheel removal, fixing a puncture ("flat") by exchanging the inner tube, and adjusting the gears and the brakes. No special tools, except two tire levers, are required for these jobs. Essentially, this section gives you a jump-start on the more detailed descriptions of all the maintenance and repair work as described in Chapters 4 to 11.

Quick-Release (QR) Operation

To remove a wheel, first release the brake. On a road bike this is done by releasing the brake tensioning quick-release lever; on a mountain bike, first unhook the connecting cable nipple.

Flip the QR lever into the "open" position.

Above: To adjust the rear derailleur, twist the adjuster at the end of the cable to tighten or slacken the derailleur cable.

Below: The brakes have a similar adjuster with which their effectiveness can be increased. On a mountain bike the adjuster is on the lever, on a road bike on the brake itself.

On the rear wheel, hold the rear derailleur while easing your wheel from its drop-outs. The chain will disengage and your derailleur will remain adjusted.

Now you can take the wheel off—if not, spin the QR lever counterclockwise once or twice while holding the locknut at the other end.

When reinstalling the wheel, make sure you adjust the locknut so that the QR lever snaps into place after overcoming noticeable resistance when twisting it into the "closed" position. Always first loosen the QR lever before tightening or loosening the locknut. For more details, see Chapter 7.

Puncture—Tube Replacement

To replace a tube, remove your wheel and place a tire lever under the tire bead, hooking it to a spoke. Hook a second tire lever under the tire bead, and slide it around the wheel's circumference.

Push the valve through the stem hole and remove the tube. Run your fingers around the inside of the tire cautiously, checking for sharp objects. Check the rim tape and be sure it covers all spokes.

Place the new tube inside the tire (which is still on the wheel), and inflate it slightly. Hook the valve under the tire bead first, then place the tire bead inside the rim. Inflate the tube, making sure the tube and the tire are seated properly. For more details, see Chapter 7.

Derailleur Adjustment

If an indexed derailleur shifts off the wheel, turn the rear cable barrel adjuster counterclockwise to increase cable tension. If the derailleur shifts into the spokes, turn the limit screw marked L in by about half a turn; if it fell off toward the right, turn the one marked H in by about half a turn. Check and repeat if necessary.

If this does not solve the problem, put the derailleur in the highest gear (smallest cog) and turn the cable adjuster in by about a full turn to release cable tension, or out to increase cable tension.

Brake Adjustments

Locate the brake cable barrel adjusters. On a mountain bike, they are located on the brake levers; on a road bike, they are on the brakes. To tighten the brakes, loosen the locknut and turn the brake cable barrel adjuster counterclockwise. To slacken the brakes, loosen the locknut and turn the brake cable barrel adjuster clockwise. Don't forget to tighten both locknuts once you have made the adjustment. For more details, see Chapter 5.

CHAPTER 2

The Tools for the Job

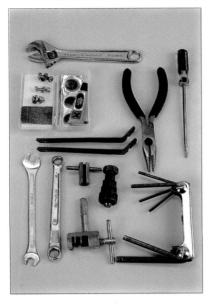

Above: A selection of tools that can easily be taken along on the bike—that also serves well as the basis of your workshop tool kit.

Below: Your next investment should include some of the items shown here, such as cone wrenches, bottom bracket tools, cable cutters, crank extractor and Allen wrenches.

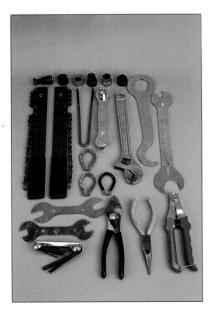

THIS chapter and the next will be devoted to very general themes. First I'll survey the most important tools required to work on the bike. In Chapter 3 I'll proceed to explain such frequently encountered details as cable adjustment, threaded connections, quick-releases and ball bearings. That same chapter also gives some guidelines for general preventive maintenance, following a simple regular schedule.

Although it's possible to spend several thousand dollars on bicycle tools, at least 90% of all maintenance and repair work can be done with a very modest outfit. And of those tools, only a few are so essential that they should be taken along on most bike trips on the road or the trail. These include universal tools that can be bought at any hardware shop, and specific bicycle tools that are available only from well-stocked bike shops or specialized mail order outlets.

Selecting Tools

Quality counts when buying tools even more than when dealing with other products. I have found quite similar-looking tools at prices that varied by a factor of three—and in my youthful ignorance I have only too often chosen the cheaper version. That's a mistake, because the tool that costs one-third as much doesn't last even a third as long. Besides, it never fits as accurately, often leading to damage both of the part handled and of the tool itself. After some unsatisfactory use, you'll probably decide to get the better tool anyway, so you finish up spending quite a bit more than you would have done buying the highest-quality tool right away.

Having sworn to buy only the best tools for the job, we can now get down to a brief description of the various essential tools of both categories—universal tools and special bicycle tools. Even more uncommon items, which are used only rarely, if at all, by the amateur bike mechanic, will be described in the chapters where their application becomes relevant.

Below, you will find most of the common tools described, some of them with an illustration. Don't be discouraged by the length of the list, since you don't really need every one of the items described here. Refer to the section on *Tools to Take Along* for the really essential tools that should be bought right away. All the other tools can wait until you have a specific need. Most bicycle components are now built with metric threading, and thus metric tool sizes will be required.

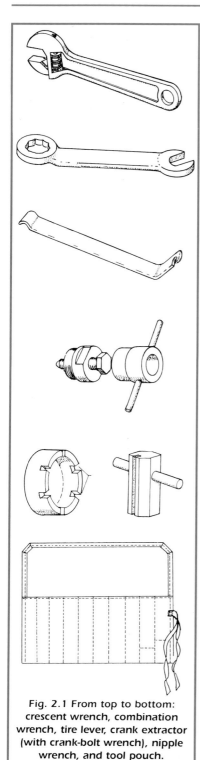

Fig. 2.1 From top to bottom: crescent wrench, combination wrench, tire lever, crank extractor (with crank-bolt wrench), nipple wrench, and tool pouch.

The size quoted in mm (millimeters) will be the dimension across flats of the point where the tool fits—not the size of the screw thread, as is customary for American and Whitworth sizes.

The specific tools to use for any one job are listed with the instructions in Chapters 4–11. However, your bike may not require each of those tools, so I recommend that you first check which are the ones needed for your bike.

Universal Tools

These are the basic tools that can be purchased in any hardware shop. I will point out which sizes are appropriate for most bicycle maintenance jobs.

Screwdriver
The screwdriver's size is designated by the blade width at the end. You will need a small one with a 4 mm (³⁄₁₆ in.) blade, a larger one with a 6–7 mm (¼–⁵⁄₃₂ in.) blade, and perhaps a Phillips-head model for screws with cross-shaped recesses instead of the conventional saw cut.

Crescent wrench
These adjustable wrenches are designated by their overall length. Get a 150 mm (6 in.) long model and one that is at least 200 mm (8 in.), perhaps even 250 mm (10 in.) long.

Box wrench
These are the most accurate tools for tightening or loosening nuts and bolts with hexagonal heads. Like all other fixed wrenches, they are designated by the across-flats dimension of the bolt on which they fit, always measured in mm. You will need sizes from 7 mm to 16 mm.

Open-ended wrench
These are the most common wrenches available. They can be used when there is not enough access room for the box wrench. Get a set in sizes from 7 mm to 16 mm.

Combination wrench
This type has a box wrench on one end and an open-ended wrench of the same size on the other. Even better than a set of each of the preceding items, get two sets of these (because for many jobs, you'll need two wrenches of the same size), again in sizes from 7 mm to 16 mm.

Allen wrench
These hexagonal L-shaped bars are used on the screws with hexagonal recesses often used on mountain bikes. They are designated by the across-flats dimension, and you will probably need these in sizes 2 mm to 9 mm. You can either get individual ones in selected sizes, or you can get a complete set. I find the latter quite handy, because individual ones tend to get lost or buried underneath other tools and parts.

Hammer
These are classified by their weight. I suggest a 300-gram (10 oz.) metalworking model, which has a head that is square at one end and wedge-shaped at the other. In addition, you may need a mallet with a plastic head of about the same weight.

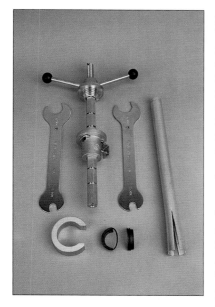

Above: The two flat wrenches are needed for headset adjustments. The other tools shown here are only needed for the more sophisticated jobs that most people would probably leave to a bike mechanic.

Below: These are the additional tools needed for high-class wheel building work: truing stand, dishing gauge, and spoke tension gauge.

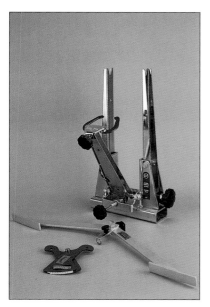

Hacksaw

When all else fails, you may find a need for one of these, e.g., to remove a tangled or rusted part or to provide a hold for the screwdriver in a damaged bolt. They are designated by their blade length. I find the 8-inch Eclipse saw quite adequate.

Files

These are designated by the length of their blade and their coarseness. Get a relatively fine 8-inch-long model to file jagged outer cable ends or remove the occasional protruding spoke or a burr at the end of a part that is cut off or damaged.

Special Bicycle Tools

The following list of tools made specifically for bicycle use includes almost all the tools you will be likely to need as a home mechanic. A much more modest selection—those listed under *Tools to Take Along*—will usually get you by when no major operations have to be carried out.

Even more specialized tools will be mentioned as we get into the actual maintenance instructions. In many cases, you will have to consult the bike shop to make sure you get the size or model of any particular tool that matches the parts installed on your bike. For that reason, it is best to have the bike with you whenever buying tools.

Pump

Although often considered an accessory, it's also an essential tool, especially on the mountain bike, since you may be riding the bike far from the nearest gas station or garage. Make sure you get a model that matches the particular valves used on your bike (Presta or Schrader, as described in Chapter 7). Many frame pumps are now equipped with both Presta and Schrader fittings. A CO_2 inflator will speed up the process, but each full tire inflation may require a new cartridge, so it's not much use except when you are racing.

Pressure gauge

In addition to the pump, I suggest you invest in a pressure gauge to make sure you inflate the tires correctly, at least to use at home—again matching the valve on your bicycle's tires.

Tire levers

These are used to lift the tire off the rim in case of a puncture or when replacing tube or tire. Select thin, flat ones that don't bend. Most mountain bike tires fit loosely enough on the rim to need only one or two, and some can actually be removed without.

Tire repair kit

The tire repair kit contains most of the other essentials for fixing a puncture, such as patches, rubber solution, and sandpaper. This little box also comes in handy to carry other small spare parts, such as duct tape for emergency repairs, extra nuts and bolts, pump washers, and light bulbs.

Spoke wrench

Also referred to as a spoke key, it is used to tighten, remove or install a spoke. Quality is especially important when purchasing

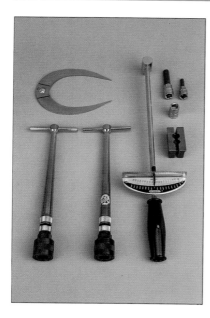

Above: Some more sophisticated tools, including frame alignment gauge and drop-out straightening tools, axle clamp, and a torque wrench to assure critical screwed connections are tightened just right.

Below: More down-to-earth is this basic collection of cleaning and lubrication aids.

these—get the individual color-coded nipple wrench that fits your spokes.

Crank bolt wrench

This tool is usually sold together with the crank extractor described below. The wrench part is needed to tighten or loosen the crank attachment bolts. Make sure you get one that matches the cranks installed on your bike, since they vary from make to make, sometimes even from model to model.

Crank extractor

This part threads into the crank center, and pulls it off the bottom bracket spindle. Once again, quality counts, so buy a good one—in the size to match the make and model of your cranks.

Freewheel tool

Used to remove a freewheel mechanism from the rear hub. This tool must be selected to match the particular freewheel used on your bike.

Chain whip (chain wrench)

This device is used to remove individual cogs from the free-

wheel. Depending on the kind of freewheel on the bike, you may either need two, or one used in conjunction with the manufacturer's special wrench.

Chain rivet tool

This tool is used to thrust out a pin in any link of the chain so it can be separated for maintenance.

Cone wrench

These very flat open-ended wrenches are used to overhaul the bearings of a wheel hub. Available in several sizes—get two of each of the sizes needed for the hubs on your bike.

Bottom bracket tools

Needed for maintenance operations on the bottom bracket bearings. Many bikes are equipped with bottom brackets that need quite specific tools for this work, so make sure to match the tools to the components on your bike.

Headset tools

These are oversize flat open-ended wrenches, used to overhaul the steering system's bearings.They are available in sizes to match different headsets.

Lubricants and Cleaning Aids

In addition to the tools listed above, you will need some materials to help you clean the bike and its parts and to lubricate for minimum friction and maximum durability. Use the following items:

Bearing grease

Either the special kind sold under the brand name of bicycle component manufacturers, such as Phil Wood or Campagnolo, or any regular lithium-based bearing grease.

Oil

Ordinary mineral oils attract too much dirt, and it is

preferable to use special bicycle lubricants such as Finish Line or Pedros.

Chain lube

Use any bicycle chain lubricant, such as Tri-Flow—or Midnght Oil for rainy weather.

Penetrating oil

A spray-can of thin, highly penetrating solvent-based

Above: Very often tools have to be used in pairs, such as here where one open-ended wrench is used to hold the bolt, and a second one to tighten or loosen the nut.

Below: Tools must have adequate leverage, and you have to find some way of applying enough force, using a fixed point to restrain your hand.

lubricant, such as WD-40 or the lightest grade of LPS to loosen things such as rusty nuts and bolts, which will come loose after they are soaked for a few minutes.

Anti-seize lubricant
This is a paste-like compound that should be applied to screw-threaded connections between steel and aluminum parts to prevent binding.

Solvents
Preferable to kerosene, there are environmentally safe citrus oil–based solvents, such as those made by Finish Line, available from many bike shops. Do not use paint thinner, since that will dissolve not only dirt and grease, but also paint and even the cement used for bonded frames and components.

Wax
Bare metal surfaces as well as painted ones are best protected with wax, applied after cleaning. Don't use regular furniture wax, since that often contains solvents that might attack the painted or aluminum surfaces.

Containers
A flat container to catch drips while lubricating or cleaning, and a jar to clean out small parts and brushes.

Cloths
You'll need at least one clean and one greasy cloth. The latter is made that way by applying bearing grease or oil—or simply after you've used it as a clean cloth for some time.

Brushes
Get two sizes of regular paint brushes, about 2 and 4 cm (¾ and 1½ in.) wide. For cleaning in tight places, the most suitable brushes are the cylindrical bottle brushes, which are also available in several sizes.

Other cleaning aids
Many cleaning jobs are done simply with a cloth and water, while some may require the use of a mixture of kerosene or another solvent with about 5%–10% mineral oil.

Tools to Take Along

Only a very limited selection of the tools listed above are so essential that you should carry them along on your rides. When cycling off-road, or whenever your road trip takes you far away from bike shops and gas stations, you should probably be more generous in what to take along than you might be when riding on paved roads in built-up areas. Under these conditions, there is not much chance of getting help on the way, let alone hitching a ride home.

The following lists just my personal preference; feel free to expand this list to suit your own needs. In addition to that, refer to the section on spare parts below for other items you may want to carry.

After you have had some experience, you may decide to expand or modify this list to include the items *you* are most comfortable with. Whatever you select, perhaps the most important thing to keep in mind is to check the types and sizes of tools that are needed for the jobs on your bike. There is no point carrying tools for equipment that is not installed on your particular bike. On the other hand, if you are

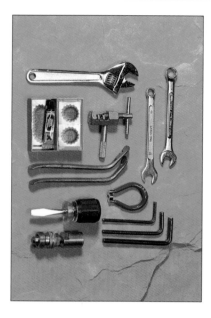

A tool kit assembled for a mountain bike trip. It includes all the tools needed—in the right sizes for any particular bike.

traveling with a group, you may decide to carry just one tool kit with the appropriate equipment for all the bikes. This makes sense on a longer tour, where every gram you carry counts and there is adequate preparation time.

Carry your tools in a bag tied to the bike (a saddle bag) or make a pouch as illustrated, carried either in a bike bag or tied directly to a frame tube or under the saddle. Select a bag that does not dangle freely; it should be strapped to the seatpost and the saddle. Here's what I suggest taking along:

pump	2, 3, 4, 5, 6 mm Allen wrenches
2 or 3 tire levers	needle-nose pliers
tire patch kit	spoke wrench
small screwdriver	chain rivet tool
6-in. crescent wrench	crank bolt wrench

CHAPTER 3

Working on the Bike

Above and below: Two ways of working on the bike. If you can't afford a full-blown workstand, as shown above, you can at least get a simple display stand (below) to hold the bike steady with the rear wheel raised off the ground while you work on it.

BEFORE proceeding to more detailed repair and maintenance instructions for particular systems and components of the bike and for specific problems, the first part of this chapter will be devoted to the techniques for handling some basic mechanisms found in many places on any bicycle. This includes screw-threaded connections in general, Bowden cables and their adjustment, as well as ball bearings and their adjustment and lubrication. The second part of this chapter will be devoted to preventive maintenance.

Threaded Connections

Many of the bicycle's parts are attached, installed and themselves constructed with screw-threaded connections—not just nuts and bolts, but many other components as well. Essentially, all threaded connections are based on the same principle: a cylindrical (male) part is threaded into a corresponding hollow (female) part by means of matching helical grooves cut into each. When the male part is threaded fully into the female, the reaction force pushes the sides of the male and female threads against one another, creating so much friction that the parts are no longer free to turn, thus keeping the connection firm.

Screw threads are designated by their nominal size, generally measured in millimeters in the bicycle industry. In addition, the pitch, or number of threads per inch, and the thread angle may vary, and finally some parts have left-hand (LH) threading, instead of the usual right-hand (RH) thread. Whereas most connections use RH threading, LH thread is found on the left pedal, as well as on a few bearing parts in the drivetrain, including bottom brackets.

Most nuts and bolts are standardized—for a given nominal diameter, they will have the same pitch and the same thread angle, and they all have RH thread. Many other bicycle components are less standardized. There are at least three different industry standards for such parts as headsets, bottom brackets and freewheels. Although virtually all American-built bikes—in fact most bikes sold in the U.S., wherever they are built—are built to the BCI (British Cycle Institute) standard dimensions, chances are you will buy a component someday that turns out to have either French or Italian threading. To avoid such mismatching, always take the part to be replaced, as well as a

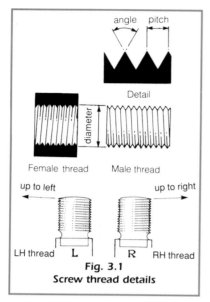

Fig. 3.1
Screw thread details

Below: Not just nuts, bolts and screws, but also many other bicycle parts, such as this headset, are connected with screw threads.

matching component to which it is threaded, to the bike shop when buying a replacement, so you can try it out there.

Whether we are talking about an ordinary nut and bolt or any other threaded part, the way to loosen and tighten the connection is the same. One part has to be restrained, while the other is turned relative to it. You turn it to the right to tighten, the left to loosen. ("rightie tightie, leftie loosie" is a popular bike shop mnemonic.) Use accurately fitting tools to give the best possible hold and to minimize damage. Use tools with adequate leverage (for example a wrench with a long handle) on the part that is turned, while the part that is merely restrained may be held with less leverage (a screwdriver or a shorter wrench).

All threaded connections should be clean and lightly greased when they are installed. If you have difficulty loosening a connection, first squirt some penetrating oil, such as WD-40, at any accessible point where the male part disappears into the female part. To allow a nut or the head of a bolt to be turned when it is tightly fastened to the part it holds, a plain washer should be installed between the two. This allows you to tighten the joint more firmly and eases disassembly as well. To prevent binding of threaded connections between steel and aluminum parts, apply some special anti-seize lubricant to the screw threads before assembly.

Many threaded connections are further secured by one means or another to minimize the chances of coming loose because of vibrations caused while riding. These are the locknut, spring washer and locking-insert nut. The locknut is a second nut that is tightened against the main nut, creating high friction forces in the threads working in opposite ways. The spring washer expands to hold the connection when vibration would otherwise loosen it; the locking-insert nut has a nylon insert that is deformed by the threading, offering the required high resistance against loosening. If you have problems with parts coming loose, you may use any of these techniques to secure them. A connection that comes loose frequently despite the use of a locking device is probably worn to the point where replacement—usually of both parts—is in order.

Nuts, bolts and screws come in several versions, each requiring specific tools. Conventional nuts and bolts have hexagonal heads and are tightened, loosened or held with either an open-ended wrench, a socket wrench, or a box wrench (preferably the latter, because it fits more accurately, with less chance of damage). Screws can have a regular straight saw cut, for use with a conventional screwdriver, or a cross-shaped, (Phillips) head, for use with a Phillips screwdriver. In recent years, more and more bicycle parts are held with Allen bolts, which have a hexagonal recess for use with an Allen wrench. As long as tools of exactly matching sizes are used—in preference to oversized and adjustable ones—and you don't apply excessive force, you should be able to tighten every connection adequately without doing damage. If you notice excessive resistance, it would be better to replace the threaded parts than to use oversize tools or brute force.

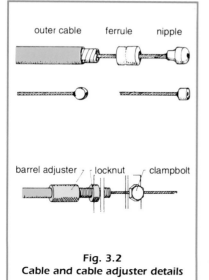

outer cable   ferrule   nipple

barrel adjuster   locknut   clampbolt

Fig. 3.2
Cable and cable adjuster details

Control Cables

Brakes and gears on the bicycle are operated via flexible Bowden cables that connect the brake or shift lever with the relevant mechanism. The inner cable transmits tension forces, which are countered by the compression forces taken up by the cable casing, also called outer cable.

The inner cable has a nipple at one end, while the other end is clamped at the brake or gear mechanism. Ferrules are installed at the ends of the cable casing to provide a firm termination at the anchor points. A new crimp should always be clamped around the free end of the inner cable to prevent fraying, or it can be soldered. There will be several different cables on your bike, and you should take care to get the right kind. In addition to the different nipple shapes in use by different makers to match particular components, the thickness can vary.

The inner cables for index gearing controls are designed to be rather stiff so that they can take up some compressive, as well as tensile, forces. The inner cables for brake controls must be quite thick to take up the high forces without stretching. Make sure the diameters of inner and outer cables are matched correctly so that the inner cable can slide through freely.

The cables for the brakes and those for conventional (non-indexed) derailleurs should be cleaned and lubricated regularly, while the ones for indexed derailleurs should only be kept clean, without lubrication. The index system invariably uses a stainless steel inner cable with a nylon sleeve between it and the inside of the casing, which makes lubrication unnecessary.

To lubricate a regular cable, you may put some grease on a cloth and run this cloth over the inner cable. Once the cable is installed, you may use spray-can lubricant, aiming with the nozzle at the points where the inner cable disappears into the casing. Remove excess lubricant with a cloth to keep things clean.

I suggest using stainless steel inner cables when replacing cables. Whether stainless or not, make sure you select them with a nipple of the same shape and size used on the original, matching the recess of the relevant lever. Some cable casings are available with a low-friction liner of either nylon or PTFE (more commonly known as Teflon); these eliminate a lot of potential maintenance problems.

Adjusting the cable tension is often necessary to adjust brakes or gears. Before attempting adjustment, make sure the cable end is clamped in firmly. To adjust, loosen the lock nut (usually a round knurled design), while restraining the adjusting barrel. Next, unscrew the adjusting barrel far enough to obtain the desired cable tension, and finally tighten the locknut while holding the adjusting barrel to restrain it.

If the length of the adjusting barrel does not allow enough adjusting range, the clamping point on the other end of the inner cable must

Below: On modern lined control cables, a low-friction nylon sleeve, or lining, sits between the inner cable and the outer cable, or cable casing.

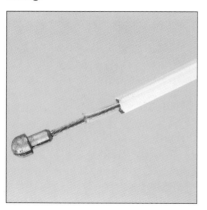

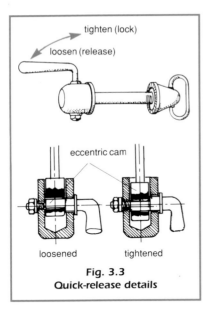

tighten (lock)
loosen (release)

eccentric cam

loosened   tightened

Fig. 3.3
Quick-release details

be moved. To do this, first back up the locknut all the way while restraining the adjusting barrel, then screw the adjusting barrel in all the way, and finally clamp the cable in a new position, while keeping it pulled taut with the aid of a pair of pliers.

Quick-Releases

Quick-release (QR) mechanisms are used on the hubs of many bikes and on the seat clamp of the mountain bike; many brakes or their levers also come equipped with some mechanism to de-tension the brake cable quickly. The quick-releases for the saddle clamp and wheel hubs work on the same principle. Instead of holding the axle or bolt by means of one or two nuts that are screwed down, a toggle lever is used.

The thumb nut at the other end is not to be used to tighten the connection, but merely to adjust it in such a way that twisting the lever tightens the whole connection firmly. Open the lever by twisting it, close it by twisting it back. If the connection does not hold, first place the lever in the open position, then tighten the thumbnut perhaps half a turn and try again. Do this until the lever not only holds the part firmly, but can also be opened enough to allow removal or adjustment of the part in question.

Recently, specialized wheel and seat clamp QR mechanisms have been introduced by some manufacturers, such as Ringle, that require a special maneuver to open and close. Other manufacturers place a retention device between the fork-end and the quick-release to prevent unintentional loosening. These devices must be flipped out of the way to release or install the wheel.

Below: Quick-releases are used on several parts on the bike. This one is used to tighten or loosen the seatpost on a mountain bike.

Ball Bearings

There are at least 14 ball bearing units in every bicycle. They are 2 each in the hubs, the headset, the pedals, the bottom bracket and the freewheel. They all work on the same principle and their condition has a great effect on the bike's performance. Understanding their operation, maintenance and adjustment is as important for every home bike mechanic as it is for the occasional cyclist who just wants to be sure his or her bike is operating optimally.

Two kinds of ball bearings are in use, the cup-and-cone, or adjustable type, and cartridge bearings (often referred to as sealed bearings). In either case, *ball bearing* does not mean one of the little balls used, but the whole assembly, while the little balls are correctly called *bearing balls*.

Although cartridge bearings are generally more accurate when new, and can be better sealed against dirt and water, they are not inherently superior. Besides, there is little maintenance you can do on these models. Either they run smoothly or they must be replaced, which generally requires special tools. Sometimes—but not usual-ly—lubrication is allowed for by means of an oil hole or a grease nipple

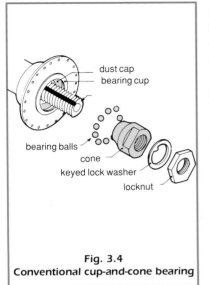

Fig. 3.4
Conventional cup-and-cone bearing

in the part in which the bearings are installed. In other cases, the best you can do is to lift off the seal with a pointed tool and apply grease.

The more common cup-and-cone bearing consists of a cone-shaped and a cup-shaped bearing race, one of which is adjustable relative to the other by means of screw threading. The bearing balls lie in the recess between these two parts and are lubricated to minimize friction. Generally, bearing grease is used as a lubricant.

Unsealed bearings should be repacked with grease at least once a year. To do it, you have to disassemble the entire bearing, as explained in the relevant chapters. Clean and inspect all parts, replacing anything that appears to be damaged (corroded, pitted or grooved). Then fill the cup-shaped bearing race with bearing grease and push the new bearing balls in, leaving enough space to allow their free movement, followed by reassembly and subsequent adjustment.

Some bearings are equipped with a system of seals and grease nipples that allow the injection of grease without it filling the entire area inside the component. These are referred to as Grease Guard and they are lubricated by injecting grease with a matching grease gun available from the same manufacturer. This method is especially suitable for mountain bike components and for bikes often ridden in wet or dusty terrain, for which repacking with grease just once a year would be inadequate.

Adjustable bearings must be so adjusted that the moving part is free to rotate with minimal friction, yet has no play or looseness. To adjust a cup-and-cone bearing, proceed as follows:

1. Loosen the locknut or lock-ring while holding the underlying cone or cup.
2. Lift the lock washer.
3. Tighten or loosen the threaded main bearing cone or cup about 1/8–1/4 turn at a time.
4. Hold the threaded cone or cup, while tightening the locknut or lockring.
5. Repeat if necessary.

Below: Detail of ball bearing retainer and spindle. Note the orientation of the bearing retainer: the metal cage goes on the side of the cone, so that the balls will project toward the bearing cup.

Workshop and Bike Support

When you are out in terrain or on the road, you can't be too picky, but when doing maintenance or repair work at home, I recommend you provide an organized workshop space. It needn't be a separate room or a permanently designated location. But while working on the bike, it should be adequately equipped for doing so.

The amount of space needed is quite modest: 7 ft. x 6 ft. (2.10 m x 1.80 m) is enough for any maintenance work ever done on the bike. As a minimum, you should equip this area with the tools and the cleaning and lubrication aids listed in the preceding chapter. In addition, you will need a workbench—although the kitchen worktop or an old table will do. Ideally, you should install a sizable metal-working vise on the workbench, although probably 98% of all the jobs described in this book can be carried out without.

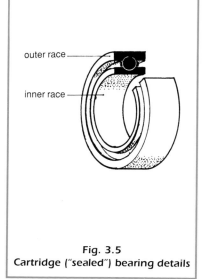

Fig. 3.5
Cartridge ("sealed") bearing details

outer race

inner race

Next, you will want a support for the bike. The best ones are freestanding devices or those mounted against the wall. I suggest you buy a bike stand that will support the bike off the ground. A simpler but adequate solution is to turn the bike upside down, supporting it at the handlebars by means of a home-made device that serves to raise the handlebars off the ground far enough to protect anything mounted there.

Mountain bikes and other models with flat handlebars can usually be placed upside down without such a support, merely turning the shifters out of the way to protect them, and that is what you will have to do when you have a problem while far from home. Just don't forget to do this each time you turn it over without adequate support, using a 5 mm Allen key to loosen the clamps that attach the shifters. Tighten them again in the proper positions when you have finished.

Buying Replacements and Tools

Whenever you have to buy a replacement part for the bike, take either the whole bike or at least the old part and one matching component (for example, the nut as well as the bolt, the handlebars as well as the stem, when replacing either one) with you to make sure you get perfectly matching components. The same goes for buying tools for specific jobs, because many makes and models of similar parts exist that may vary in size, each requiring its own matching tool.

Preventive Maintenance

Test the brakes by trying to push the bike forwards while pulling the brake levers individually and applying your weight to the bike.

At the risk of being trite, I must emphasize that in bicycle maintenance, an ounce of prevention is worth a pound of repairs. Preventive maintenance will eliminate the vast majority of unanticipated repairs later on. When problems do develop, try to take care of them immediately, rather than wait until they are so serious that they become difficult to fix due to additional damage. It's all a matter of knowing what to look for and how to put it right.

Keep your bike clean; you will find it much easier both to spot problems and to work on the bike. Regularly check to make sure every nut and bolt is tight and nothing is damaged. Don't leave your bike out in the rain, but if it's unavoidable, wipe the bike clean and dry immediately to prevent rust and dirt build-up.

Although most of the actual maintenance operations are covered in detail in the chapters that follow, this is the time to get familiar with a systematic schedule to check the bike. Good preventive maintenance is based on a system of (almost) daily, monthly and annual checks, proceeding as outlined below. These are merely lists of jobs that need to be done; for the actual instructions telling you exactly how to go about it, and what to do to correct any problems you encounter, refer to the individual chapters that follow, each of which deals with a particular system or group of components on the bike.

Above: Make sure the wheels are held firmly in the drop-outs —especially the front wheel, because spontaneous front wheel release can lead to serious accidents.

Below: Make sure the handlebars are tightened firmly, by clamping the front wheel between your legs and trying to twist the handlebars.

Daily Inspection

This may seem to be overdoing it a little, but there are a few things you ought to look out for whenever you take the bike out. These will be covered in this section.

☐ **Quick-Release Mechanisms**:
Check quick-release mechanisms on wheels.

☐ **Tires**:
Check whether the tires are inflated properly, considering the type of terrain you will ride in: 90–105 psi (6–7 bar) for a racing bike on smooth roads; 60–75 psi (4–5 bar) for touring bikes, mountain bikes, hybrids and even mountain bikes on smooth, hard roads; 45 psi (3 bar) for mountain bikes on rough but hard surfaces; 30 psi (2 bar) for mountain bikes on loose and irregular surfaces.

☐ **Handlebars**:
Make sure the handlebars are straight, at the right height, and cannot be easily twisted from side to side.

☐ **Saddle**:
Verify that the saddle is straight, level, securely attached to the seatpost and at the right height.

☐ **Brakes**:
Check the effectiveness of the brakes by verifying that each can block the wheel against your weight pushing the bike forward with the lever depressed, leaving about 2 cm (¾ in.) between brake lever and handlebars.

☐ **Gears**:
Lift the rear wheel and, while turning the cranks, check whether the derailleurs can be shifted to reach every combination of chainring and cog. However, avoid combining the largest chainring with the largest cog, or the smallest chainring with the smallest cog.

Monthly Inspection

At least once a month during the time you use the bike, clean it as as described on page 30. Then carry out the same inspections listed above for the daily inspection, and in addition do the following:

☐ **Wheels**:
Check for broken spokes and wheel wobble. Lift the wheel off the ground and turn it relatively slowly, keeping an eye on a fixed point such as the brake pads. If the wheel seems to wobble sideways relative to the fixed point, it should be trued.

☐ **Brakes**:
Observe what happens when you pull the brake levers forcefully. The brake pads must touch the side of the rim over their entire surface when the lever is pulled hard. Adjust the brake as outlined in Chapter 5 if they don't.

Above: When removing the rear wheel, keep the chain out of the way—ideally, the bike should have a little stop on the inside of the RH seat stay to hold the chain, as shown here.

Below: This is the way to clean between and around the cogs on the rear wheel.

☐ **Tires:**
Check the tires for external damage and embedded objects. Remove anything that doesn't belong there and replace the tire if necessary.

☐ **Cranks**:
Using the crank extractor tool, tighten the crank attachment nuts or bolts, as explained in Chapter 7.

☐ **General inspection**:
Check all the other bolts and nuts to make sure they are tight. Verify whether all moving parts turn freely and all adjustments are correct. Repair or replace anything damaged or missing.

Lubrication

Lubricate the small moving parts, using the lubricants indicated below. Wipe off any excess.

☐ **Chain:** Use special chain lube.

☐ **Exposed uncoated metal parts:** Use bicycle polish or car wax.

☐ **Brake levers, pivots, cables:** Spray a light lubricant, aiming precisely with the little tubular nozzle installed on the spray head.

Annual Inspection

The work described below will be necessary at least once a year, twice a year if you ride a lot in bad weather both in summer and winter. This is a complete overhauling job, which very nearly returns the bike to its as-bought condition. Treated this way, your bike will last a lifetime.

If you use the bike only in the fair-weather period, carry out this work at the end of the season. Then merely carry out a monthly inspection at the beginning of the next season. During the annual inspection, proceed as follows:

☐ First carry out all the work described above for the monthly inspection, noting in particular which parts need special attention because they seem to be loose, worn, damaged or missing. Subsequently, work down the following list.

☐ **Wheels:**
With the wheels still on the bike, check for damage to the rim or the tire and for loose or missing spokes.

Then take the wheel out and overhaul the hubs, as described in Chapter 7, repacking them with bearing grease. This work is not necessary if the hubs have cartridge bearings, as long as they are operating perfectly smoothly and without play. It is a good idea to put a drop of light oil, such as Tri-Flow, under the cartridge bearing seal.

Above: Inflate the tires properly, holding the pump head perpendicular to the valve stem.

Below: Lubricate pivot points, and wipe off any excess oil afterwards to help keep the bike clean.

☐ **Hubs:**
Check the hubs for play, wear and tightness as explained in Chapter 7. Preferably, dismantle and lubricate or overhaul the hubs.

☐ **Chain:**
Remove the chain and measure the length of a 100-link section (the distance between the first and the fiftieth pin). Replace the entire chain if it measures more than 51 in. (129.5 cm). The apparent stretch is a sign of wear that will affect shifting and transmission efficiency. In addition, the worn chain will also wear out the chainrings and the sprockets. If you replace the chain, you may have to replace one or more sprockets as well. If the chain is not badly worn, merely rinse it out in solvent, after which it should be lubricated and reinstalled, following the instructions in Chapter 6.

☐ **Bottom bracket:**
Check it for play and freedom of rotation. If the bottom bracket is of the adjustable type, remove the crank and disassemble and overhaul the bearings as explained in Chapter 6. If it has cartridge bearings and does not spin properly, get it replaced at the bike shop or replace it yourself.

☐ **Headset:**
Try it out and make sure it rotates without play or rough spots. Preferably, disassemble and overhaul the bearings as described in Chapter 8.

☐ **Derailleurs:**
With the chain removed, clean, check and lubricate both derailleur mechanisms, making sure the pivots work smoothly and the little wheels (or pulleys) of the rear derailleur turn freely. On mountain bikes, the upper pulley is often worn, due to accumulated dirt and debris,

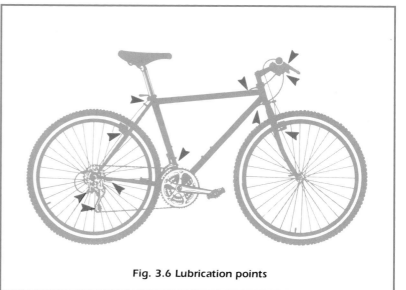

Fig. 3.6 Lubrication points

Above and below: Use the end of a cleaning cloth, wrapped around a screwdriver if necessary, to get between all the tight places on the bike.

so it must be replaced. If necessary, overhaul or

replace parts as explained in Chapter 4.

Cleaning the Bike

Do this job whenever your bike gets dirty—at least once a month in clean terrain and dry weather, much more frequently in bad weather or muddy terrain.

Cleaning procedure:

1. If the bike is dry, wipe it with a soft brush or a cloth to remove any dust and other dry dirt. If the bike—or the dirt that adheres to it—is wet, hose or sponge it down with plenty of clean water. Take care not to get the water into the hubs, pedals, bottom bracket or headset bearings, though. The same goes for a leather saddle.

2. Using a damp cloth or a toothbrush, clean all the hard-to-reach nooks and crannies. Make sure you get into all the hidden places, such as between the cogs and chainrings, underneath the brake arms, or at the derailleur pulleys.

3. Clean and dry the same areas with a clean, soft, dry cloth.

4. With a clean wax- or grease-soaked cloth, treat all the bare metal areas very sparingly to inhibit rust.

5. Twice a year, it may be worthwhile to apply a special waxy polish (either car wax or any special bicycle polish, such as Klasse) to the paintwork.This same treatment is also recommended for bare metal surfaces.

CHAPTER 4

The Gearing System

Above: The derailleur does what the name implies—it derails the chain from one cog to another.

NOWADAYS, most adult bikes are equipped with derailleur gears, although hub gearing is still used on some bikes. The derailleur system comprises a front derailleur, also called a changer, and a rear derailleur. Both are operated by means of shift levers that are mounted either on the handlebars or on the downtube. The shifters are connected to the derailleurs by means of flexible Bowden cables. The rear derailleur moves the chain sideways from one cog, or sprocket, to another on the freewheel attached to the rear wheel hub, while the front derailleur moves the chain sideways from one chainring to another.

On hub-geared bikes, there is a shifter on the handlebars, which is connected to a mechanism contained in the rear wheel hub. Hub gearing is commonly available as 2-speed, 3-speed and 5-speed systems, but even 7-speed hubs have been introduced.

Derailleur System Overview

Since the various cogs and chainrings have different numbers of teeth, varying the combination achieves a lower or higher gear. A low gear is achieved by selecting a small chainring in the front and a big cog in the rear. A high gear results when a large chainring on the front is combined with a small cog in the rear.

Below: In the highest gear, left, the chain engages the largest chainring in the front and the smallest cog in the rear. In the lowest gear, right, it engages the smallest chainring and the largest cog.

Virtually all newer bikes with derailleurs come equipped with indexed gearing. That means that there are distinct stops on the shift levers for each of the gears, eliminating the need for sensitive adjustments

Above: The rear derailleur's range of lateral movement is limited or expanded by means of the two set-stop screws. They are usually marked H and L for high and low gear range, respectively.

Below: The front derailleur's range is adjusted the same way.

when shifting. For mountain bike use, there are two major types of shift levers, mounted on top of and under the handlebars respectively. Hybrids and touring bikes with drop handlebars are often equipped with bar-end shifters, while grip shifters are also available.

For road bikes, several manufacturers have introduced gear shifters integrated in the brake levers, such as Shimano's SIS system. By and large, these systems are maintained and adjusted just like any other indexed derailleur system. The integrated brake-and-gear levers are one unit, so you'll have to replace the entire lever unit if either the brake lever or the gear shifter is damaged beyond repair.

This chapter will describe all maintenance operations necessary to maintain and adjust the gearing system and its individual components. I advise purchasing a shifter that is made by the same manufacturer as the derailleur, which in turn will work best on a matching freewheel.

Adjust Derailleur Range

The most frequently occurring derailleur problem requiring maintenance is that one of the derailleurs either exceeds its full range or fails to reach it. Another common problem is when indexed shifting doesn't work properly, and the chain gets stuck between the chainrings or cogs.

Tools and equipment:
small screwdriver   cloth

Procedure:

1. Establish the nature of your problem:
   – front or rear derailleur
   – too far or not far enough
   – left or right

2. If necessary, put the chain back on the chainring or the cog, operating the shift lever to position the derailleur if necessary.

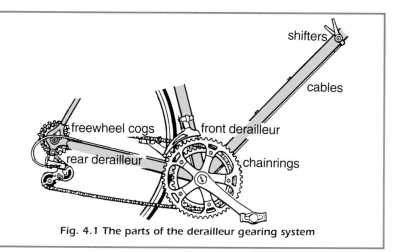

Fig. 4.1 The parts of the derailleur gearing system

Above: Adjusting the rear derailleur by means of the cable adjuster. On some models, the shifters are equipped with a similar adjuster.

Below: Typical modern rear derailleur. This is a long-cage model intended for widely spaced gears.

3. Observe how each derailleur is equipped with two set-stop screws, the ones with a little spring under the head, and usually marked with an H and an L for high and low gear, respectively. Tightening one of these screws limits the range of the derailleur in the appropriate direction. Loosening the same screw extends derailleur travel.

5. If the chain has come off on the RH side (outside, or high gear) on the front, tighten the screw marked H of the front derailleur by one turn.

6. If the chain does not quite reach the last gear on that side, loosen the screw by about that much.

7. Check all the gears, turning the cranks with the rear wheel lifted off the ground. Readjust as necessary.

Note:
If problems persist, the derailleur hanger may be bent. If so, get it straightened.

The Rear Derailleur

Indexed mechanisms are almost always used on modern bikes, and generally set up to select one of 5, 6, 7 or 8 cogs. The RH shifter has a ratchet device that corresponds with specific settings of the rear derailleur, which in turn correspond with the positions of the individual cogs.

In the case of downtube and over-the-bar shifters, there is usually a small selection lever to switch from the indexed mode to the so-called friction mode (actually just a finer ratchet), which allows the selection of intermediate positions. This is essential when the derailleur is no longer adjusted properly, allowing the selection of the right gear, especially for people who are not familiar with making derailleur adjustments. On or off-road, this will be your quick solution to any gearing problems that develop, since exact adjustment is more easily carried out at home. The index and friction modes are usually identified by the letters I and F, respectively, marked on the shifter.

Adjust Rear Derailleur

Most gearing problems can be eliminated by some form of derailleur adjustment. But first make sure the pulleys are not clogged with dirt.

Tools and equipment:
small screwdriver

5 mm Allen wrench
8 mm wrench

Procedure:

1. To get by until you have time to do a more thorough adjusting job, select the friction mode on the RH shifter (If this option is available on the shifters in question— unfortunately, that is not the case on SIS systems).

Above: Shimano Dura-Ace rear derailleur in the position for the largest cog, seen from behind.

Below: Campagnolo Chorus road bike rear derailleur set to engage the smallest cog, seen from the side.

2. Adjust the cable tension, using the built-in adjusting barrel.

3. Shift the rear derailleur to the highest gear (smallest cog) while holding the bike's rear wheel off the ground. Shift the front derailleur to the largest chainring. Use your hand to turn the cranks to engage the chain in that gear (or the closest one to it).

4. Tighten or loosen the barrel to either release or increase tension on the cable. If the cable is too loose, you will notice this now.

5. If the range of the adjusting barrel is inadequate, the cable must be clamped in at a different point. Screw the adjusting barrel in all the way, loosen the eye bolt or clamp nut that holds the cable at the derailleur, pull the cable from the end until it is taut but not under tension, and tighten the clamp nut or eye bolt again.

6. Try out all the gears and readjust the range if necessary, following the description above.

7. Now the derailleur operates correctly in friction mode. The next step will be to fine-tune the indexing. To do that, first with the shifter still set in the friction mode, select the lowest gear (biggest cog in the rear, combined with smallest chainring in the front) and make sure it achieves this gear correctly.

8. Select the highest gear again (largest chainring, smallest cog), then put the shifter in index mode, marked with the letter I.

9. Adjust the cable tension until the chain runs smoothly without scraping against the derailleur cage or the next larger cog.

10. Move the shifter one notch for the next lower gear in the back, engaging the second smallest cog if it is adjusted correctly.

11. If the derailleur does not move the chain to the next cog, tighten the cable by about one half turn of the adjusting barrel.

12. If the derailleur shifts past this second smallest cog, loosen the cable tension with the adjusting barrel by about half a turn.

13. Repeat steps 10 through 12 until the derailleur works smoothly in these two gears.

14. With the derailleur set for the second smallest cog, tighten the cable with the adjusting barrel just so far that the chain runs noisily, scraping against the third smallest cog.

15. Loosen the cable tension until the noises are subdued to achieve the optimal setting.

16. Ride the bicycle and attempt to shift all gears to verify correct adjustments.

Notes:

☐ If adjusting does not solve the problem, first replace the cable and cable casing. File the newly cut cable casing end flush.

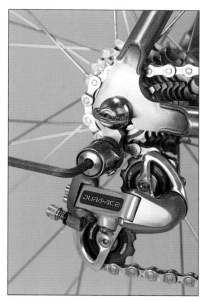

Above: The rear derailleur is installed on the RH rear drop-out by means of a 6 mm Allen bolt.

Below: To open up the cage and remove a pulley, or to release the chain, unscrew the bolt that runs through the lower, or tension, pulley.

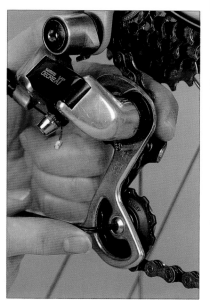

Nowadays, most rear derailleurs have a third adjusting screw, which is used to adjust the angle of the deraileur. Select the gear in which the chain runs on the biggest cog, and adjust it so that the chain comes close to it, without the cog scraping the pulley.

Many new mountain bikes with under-the-bar shifters also have a cable adjustment that is located next to the shifter's ratchet. It should be tightened before attempting a rear cable adjustment.

Overhaul Rear Derailleur

This work will be necessary when so much dirt has built up that operation of the mechanism has become unreliable and can not be solved by adjusting.

Tools and equipment:
3 mm Allen wrench
7 mm open-ended wrench
solvent
cloths
grease
spray lubricant
2 small crescent wrenches

Procedure:

1. Remove the bolts at the little wheels (called the tension and jockey pulley, respectively) over which the chain runs, catching the wheels, bushings and bolts.

2. Clean the wheels and the bushings inside, as well as all other parts of the mechanism that are more easily accessible now.

3. If the pulleys appear to be worn, take them to a bike shop and buy new ones. Although they look alike, they do differ—on many models the tension pulley even differs from the jockey pulley—so exact replacements are necessary.

4. If the cage is bent, carefully straighten it using two crescent wrenches—one on either side of the bend.

5. If you are ambitious, continue disassembly only if the mechanism cannot be cleaned adequately without doing so. Before removing the hinged cage, visualize how the internal spring works, so you will be able to reinstall it correctly. If necessary, you can increase the spring tension by placing the end in a different notch. If you are less ambitious, take it to a bike shop.

6. Lubricate the bushings in the pulleys with grease and all pivots with light oil, wiping off any excess.

7. Reassemble the chain cage with the pulley, guiding the chain through the cage.

8. Try out all the gears and adjust the derailleur if necessary.

Above: Detail showing disassembly and installation of the rear derailleur pulley.

Center and bottom: Attaching the derailleur cable. Use needle-nose pliers to pull the cable taut before clamping it in firmly.

Replace Rear Derailleur

This is done when the derailleur must be replaced because its operation cannot be restored by adjusting or replacing parts. Generally, a short-cage derailleur can be used—regardless what the manufacturer had originally installed, providing the largest rear cog does not exceed 28 teeth. They work more predictably and are less fragile than the long-cage versions, while also reducing chain slack.

Tools and Equipment:

chain rivet extractor
5 mm Allen wrench

small screwdriver
cloth
grease

Removal Procedure:

1. If you prefer to leave the chain intact, open up the cage by removing the bolt of the jockey pulley.

2. Otherwise, separate the chain using the chain rivet tool.

3. Cut the cable crimp, undo the cable attachment and catch the ferrules and cable casing.

4. Undo the derailleur attachment bolt and remove the derailleur.

Installation Procedure:

1. The new derailleur must be compatible with the shifter and the freewheel installed on the bike. For example, if you have a 7- or 8-speed system, you need a derailleur with enough travel for that distance.

2. Clean and grease the derailleur eye threads, and gently screw in the derailleur. Put the new derailleur in the same location as the old one was, checking to make sure it pivots freely around the mounting bolt.

3. Attach the cable.

4. Either install the chain (if it had been removed) or open up the cage by removing the bolt of the jockey pulley to put the chain in place, then reinstall the guide wheel.

5. Try out all the gears and adjust the derailleur and the cable tension if necessary.

The Front Derailleur

Although many mountain bike front derailleurs, or changers, are indexed, requiring a matching indexed shifter, road bikes are usually equipped with non-indexed models, because there are only 2 chainrings to choose from.

The major maintenance work on the front derailleur is the range adjusting procedure described above. In addition, the cable tension can be adjusted similarly to that for the rear derailleur when it does not shift properly. Most front derailleurs used for road bikes do not

Above: This is the correct location for the front derailleur. This photo also shows how the set-stop screws are adjusted.

Below: Pull the front derailleur cable taut before clamping it in.

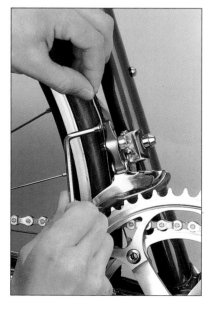

have a cable adjuster built into the cable casing. In that case, any adjustments have to be made by repositioning the clamp on the inner cable.

Adjust Front Derailleur

This job must be done when the front derailleur "dumps" the chain by the side of the chainrings, when one chainring cannot be reached, or when the chain scrapes on the derailleur cage.

Tools and equipment:
5 and 6 mm Allen wrenches   small screwdriver

Procedure:

1. First make sure the derailleur cage is perfectly parallel to the chainrings. If it needs adjustment, loosen the attachment bolt and twist the derailleur into position before retightening.

2. Carry out any adjustment of the set-stop screws that may be necessary.

3. Set the shifter in the position for the highest gear with the chain on the large outside chainring.

4. In this position, the cable should be just taut, though not under tension.

5. If necessary, tighten or loosen it by clamping the cable in at a different point. Loosen the eye bolt or clamp nut with either the 5 mm Allen wrench or 8 mm wrench, pull the cable taut and tighten the eye bolt or clamp nut again.

6. Check all gears and make any other adjustments that may be necessary.

Replace Front Derailleur

This may become necessary if the mechanism is bent or damaged—usually as the result of a fall.

Tools and equipment: small screwdriver
5 or 6 mm Allen wrench   chain rivet extractor

Removal Procedure:

1. Loosen the cable attachment by unscrewing the eye bolt or the clamp nut, and pull the cable end out.

2. Either remove the chain with the chain rivet extractor or, on some models, you can open up the derailleur's chain guide cage by removing the little bolt through the bushing that connects the two sides in the back of the cage.

3. Undo the attachment bolt.

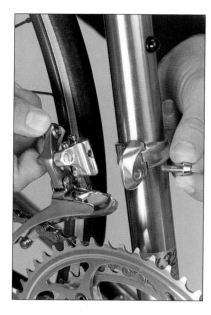

Above: Installing the front derailleur by means of a clamp. On some bikes the clamp is replaced by a brazed-on lug attached to the seat tube, as shown in the photo on page 37.

Below: Tighten the derailleur mounting bolt, or the clip bolt, after the derailleur has been perfectly positioned and aligned.

Installation Procedure:

1. Install the derailleur on the seat tube, with the cage parallel to the chainrings. Don't tighten it solidly yet.

2. Fine-tune the position, leaving a distance of 2–4 mm ($\frac{3}{32}$–$\frac{3}{16}$ in.) clearance between the largest chainring and the bottom of the cage, making sure it is aligned. Now tighten the attachment bolt fully.

3. Feed the cable through the derailleur as shown, and attach it in the eye bolt or under the clamp nut.

4. Adjust the cable tension so that it is just taut, but not under tension, with the shifter set for the highest gear and the chain on the largest chainring.

5. Check all the gears and adjust the derailleur range if necessary.

The Shifters

If the shifter does not work properly, and the derailleur jumps out of the selected gear, the reason may be a damaged or corroded derailleur cable. First check the cable, and replace it and perhaps the cable casing, if necessary.

If the cable and the derailleur themselves are working properly, the problem may be due to either insufficient tension on the spring inside the derailleur, dirt, corrosion, or wear of the notched ring inside. Only in the latter case will it be necessary to replace the shifter.

First try cleaning and tensioning the shifter. Do not attempt to take your shifter apart unless it is a friction shifter. If it is, you can take it apart carefully and note where the various bits and pieces go. Then clean and lightly lubricate all parts with grease. Finally reassemble and if necessary turn the screw that holds it all together a little tighter.

Replace Shifter

If the shifter cannot be made to work by means of adjustment and cable replacement, it can easily be replaced.

Tools and equipment:
5 mm Allen wrench

small screwdriver
8 mm wrench

Removal Procedure:

1. Undo the inner cable clamp at the derailleur.

2. Remove the shifter attachment screw.

3. Pull the inner cable out and catch the cable casing and any loose items.

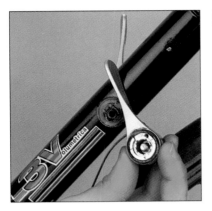

Top: Modern downtube-mounted shifters, as used on road bikes, include an indexing ratchet.

Center: SIS integrated brake-and-gear levers on a road bike.

Bottom: Many mountain bikes have double shifters mounted under the handlebars. Again, note the indexing ratchet.

Installation Procedure:

1. Attach the shifter in the desired location.

2. Feed the cable through the shifter with the nipple in the recess.

3. Guide the cable through the various guides and the cable casing, and attach the end at the derailleur.

4. Adjust the derailleur cable tension.

Note:
Shimano STI and Campagnolo Ergopower shifters are combined with the brake levers. They are installed, removed and replaced together with the brake levers. This procedure is illustrated and described in Chapter 5.

Derailleur Cables

Indexed shifters rely on relatively stiff stainless steel inner cables and a nylon sleeve between the inner cable and cable casing. These same cables can also be used on non-indexed systems. They only need to be cleaned from time to time and checked to make sure they are not pinched or damaged anywhere. Other cables (without the nylon sleeve) must also be lubricated from time to time. This is best done by removing them and smearing grease over the inner cable. If you don't want to remove the cable, squirt a few drops of oil between the cable and the cable casing at the ends where the inner cable disappears in the casing.

Replace Derailleur Cable

This work is necessary if the cable is pinched or otherwise damaged, or if the inner cable shows signs of corrosion or frayed strands. If you have under-the-bar shifters, the cable must match the shifter, since the two major manufacturers (SunTour and Shimano) use different nipples.

Tools and equipment:
5 mm Allen wrench
8 mm wrench

cable cutters
screwdriver
file

Removal Procedure:

1. Undo the cable at the derailleur by loosening the cable clamp nut or the eye bolt that holds the cable to the derailleur.

2. Put the shifter in the position for the highest gear.

3. On under-the-bar shifters, open up the mechanism only to the point where the cable and the nipple are exposed.

4. Push the cable free at the shifter.

5. Pull the cable out and catch the cable casing and any other loose items such as cable end caps and ferrules.

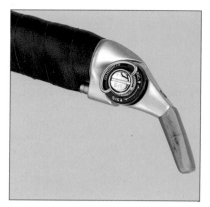

Top: On bar-end shifters, the gear cable is routed under the handlebar tape.

Center: Many recent shift levers have an indicator to show the gear.

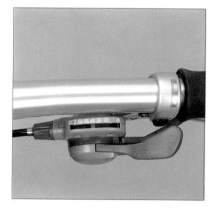

Bottom: On some derailleur systems, there is a tensioning toggle for the gear cable mounted on the downtube.

Installation Procedure:

1. Grease the cable, and file the cable casing ends if it is a replacement.

2. Feed the cable through the shifter as shown, with the nipple in the recess. If there is a nipple at both ends, cut off the one that you won't use.

3. Guide the inner cable through the various guides and stops on the frame and the cable casing, then thread it through the derailleur clamp. Apply gentle torque once correct tension is established.

4. After you have established the correct cable length and have adjusted the tension, crimp or solder the strands of the inner cable end together to prevent fraying.

Twistgrip Shifter

These devices are mainly used on some entry-level mountain bikes and hybrids. However, they are suitable for retrofitting as a replacement for conventional shifters. The GripShift works with any Shimano or SunTour derailleur, while the Campagnolo and Sachs models only work well with the same manufacturer's derailleurs.

Procedure

1. Follow the instructions for cable removal above, and then remove the old shifter and the handgrip.

2. Hook the cable nipple in the recess and route the cable through from inside, keeping the cable casing in place.

3. Install the twistgrip like any other handgrip, but tighten it with the clamping screw when it is in such a location that the numbers are visible from the rider's position.

4. Route the cable to the derailleur and clamp it in, keeping the cable casing taut.

5. Put the twistgrip shifter in the position for the highest gear and clamp in the end. Adjust the derailleur until the cable is taut.

6. Adjust the cable tension until all the gears work properly.

Hub Gearing

Since the introduction of indexed shifters for derailleur bikes, hub gearing has been on the decline. However, recent developments suggest this method will be making a comeback. It is now available with anywhere up to 7 gears. Most hub gear systems are operated by means of a handlebar-mounted shifter which control the hub's internal selector mechanism via one or two flexible cables that run over rollers or guides.

Above: Twistgrip shifters are gaining in popularity. First used on entry-level hybrids, they have meanwhile improved far enough to use on high-end mountain bikes.

Below: The twistgrip is positioned and aligned with a 2 mm Allen wrench.

The hub axle is hollow and carries the selector rod on which the clutch mechanism is held. On most models, the selector rod is attached to a little chain, while other models connect it with a hinge mechanism screwed on in the location of the axle nut. The cable is attached to the little chain or the hinge by means of a cable adjuster which serves to correct the adjustment of the gears. When shifting toward a lower gear, the rod is pulled farther out and sets the selector in the appropriate position.

The 2-speed gear, used mainly for portable bicycles, works without external controls: it is operated by pedaling backwards.

Hub Gear Maintenance

Whenever hub gearing does not work properly, it is generally not due to the mechanism itself, but rather to the controls. Slipped cable guides or pinched cables are the most frequent causes of control problems. Consequently, these points should be checked before attempting to adjust the mechanism.

Most models made by Sachs are lubricated for life and only break down when the hub overheats on models with a coaster brake built in. In that case, the hub should be disassembled and the bearings repacked with the manufacturer's special grease. Most other models are equipped with an oil nipple and should be lubricated with 10 drops of light oil once every three months or whenever the hub appears not to run or shift smoothly. On 3-speed models, the coaster brake can be eliminated by disassembling the unit and removing the sectioned, cylindrical brake mantle with the brake cone.

To date, Sturmey-Archer's models with built-in drum brakes are not equipped with a seal that separates the brake from the gears. The result is that when the bike lies on its left side, the oil from the gears enters the brake drum where it ruins the brake shoes. Consequently, the manufacturer delivers the hub unlubricated. Lubricate such a hub before use—and don't put the bike down in such a way that it rests on its LH side.

Adjust Sturmey-Archer 3-Speed Hub

On these hubs, the cable is connected to a tiny chain that comes out of the RH axle nut. The correct adjustment can be checked based on the alignment seen through a viewing port in this nut. Generally, no tools are required, although a pair of pliers may be needed if the adjuster is too tight.

Procedure:

1. Establish whether the cable and any rollers are in order, and the stops and guides are attached properly. Correct if necessary.

2. If the hub has not been lubricated for more than 3 months, first lubricate it through the oil hole, then turn the cranks several

Hub gear detail, showing the control cable and its adjusting mechanism on a Sturmey-Archer 3-speed.

times in each gear with the wheel lifted off the ground.

3. Place the shift lever in the normal gear position (N or 2), while turning the cranks at least half a revolution.

4. Check the situation through the viewing port in the RH axle nut. The hub is correctly adjusted if the shoulder on the internal pin to which the chain is connected is exactly aligned with the end of the wheel axle (move the shift lever back and forth a little to check).

5. To adjust the cable adjuster, loosen the locknut, turn the internally threaded bushing relative to the threaded pin, then hold in position while tightening the locknut.

6. Check and readjust if necessary.

Adjust Sachs 3-Speed Hub

Models made since about 1975 do not have a neutral position. Consequently, the problem here never shows as loss of transmission, but merely by the fact that a different gear from the one selected remains engaged. The adjustment is done in the high gear, and no tools are required.

Procedure:

1. Establish whether the cable, its guides and stops, and the shifter all operate correctly and the stops and guides are not loose. Correct if necessary.

2. Place the shift lever in the high gear position (H or 3), while turning the cranks at least half a revolution.

3. Adjust the special cable adjuster, which is simply clamped on a serrated rod. Push the clip in, slide it up or down, holding the serrated rod in the other hand, until the cable is just taut but not under tension, and let go of the clip.

4. Check and readjust if necessary.

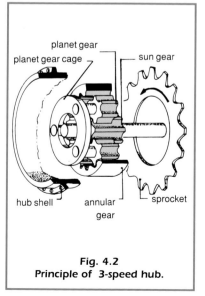

planet gear
planet gear cage
sun gear
hub shell
annular gear
sprocket

**Fig. 4.2
Principle of 3-speed hub.**

Adjust Shimano 3-Speed Hub

On these hubs, the controls are carried via a bell crank, or hinge mechanism, on the LH side of the hub. This hinge mechanism has an integral locknut and must be positioned so that the pivoting movement is fully aligned with the cable. To achieve this, you may have to loosen the locknut a little, adjust the bell crank to the right position, and then hold it there while tightening the locknut. Generally, no tools will be required for the rest of the work.

Procedure:

1. Check whether the cable, its guides and stops, the

bell crank, and the shifter all operate correctly and the

Above: This is how you replace the 3-speed hub's shifter cable.

Below: The cog of the hub gear can be replaced by a smaller or bigger one to achieve a higher or a lower range of gears, respectively. To do that, remove the spring clip with a small screwdriver, then lift the cog off. Use needle-nose pliers to reinstall the clip.

stops, guides and bell crank are properly attached. Correct if necessary.

2. Place the shift lever in the high gear position (N or 2), while turning the cranks at least half a revolution.

3. If the gears are correctly adjusted, the letter N or the number 2 should now be completely visible in the window in the bell crank.

4. If it is not, adjust the cable adjuster attached to the bell crank until the number is visible in the window.

5. Check each of the gears in turn while turning the cranks with the wheel lifted, and re-adjust if necessary.

5-Speed Hubs

These units include a double set of planet gears inside, each with its own controls. They are available from Sturmey-Archer and Sachs. The one made by Sturmey-Archer is available with and without a built-in drum brake. Sachs makes versions without a brake, with a cable-operated drum brake and with a coaster brake.

Recent models are operated by a single lever that controls the two cables (older models had two separate levers). Unfortunately, these shifters are made of a relatively soft fiber-reinforced plastic which deforms easily, especially at the point where the cable nipple is held. A lot of problems are prevented by taking the unit apart early in its life and applying a generous amount of the special grease specified by the manufacturer to everything that moves. If nothing else will do the trick, you'll have to replace the entire shifter.

Adjust Sturmey-Archer 5-Speed Hub

On most versions of this hub, there is a bell crank mechanism on the LH side, while the RH side has the same nut with viewing port as found on the same manufacturer's 3-speed models. Verify whether the cable runs freely, the cable stops are firmly installed, and whether the bell crank and the control chain are exactly aligned with their respective cable sections. If the hub has not been lubricated in the last 3 months, do that first, after which it should be tried again. Once these points have been corrected, no tools are required as a rule.

Procedure for models with two separate shifters:

1. Place the LH shifter in the position that releases tension on the LH cable, while turning the cranks at least half a revolution with the wheel lifted off the ground.

2. If necessary, adjust it so that it is just taut but not under tension.

3. Place the RH shifter in the intermediate position.

4. Check to make sure the cable is tensioned fully with

Close-up of 5-speed hub gear, showing the control chain and adjustment mechanism. The Sachs unit shown here relies on a simple clip connector, instead of the barrel adjuster still used by Sturmey-Archer.

the slightest shift of the LH shifter.

5. Check all gears. If any do not work, adjust the RH adjuster a little looser or tighter.

Procedure for models with a single shifter:

1. Select the fourth gear.

2. Adjust the RH mechanism as described for the same manufacturer's 3-speed hub.

3. Place the shifter in the position for the fifth gear while turning the cranks half a revolution with the wheel raised off the ground.

4. The LH cable should now be tightened—adjust, if necessary.

5. Try out all the gears and readjust, if necessary.

Adjust Sachs 5-Speed Hub

This hub is always operated by means of a single shifter. No tools are needed for the adjustment, which has to be preceded by the usual check of the cables, shifter, guide and stops. If an old model has persistent shifter problems, replace the shifter.

Procedure:

1. Select the fifth gear while turning the cranks forward with the wheel raised off the ground.

2. Loosen the cable adjusting clips on both sides, so the cables on both sides of the hub are completely loose in this position.

3. Turn the cranks forward by at least one revolution with the wheel raised off the ground.

4. Put the cable adjusting clips on their pins so that the cables are just taut but not under tension.

5. Select the first gear while turning the cranks forward with the wheel raised off the ground.

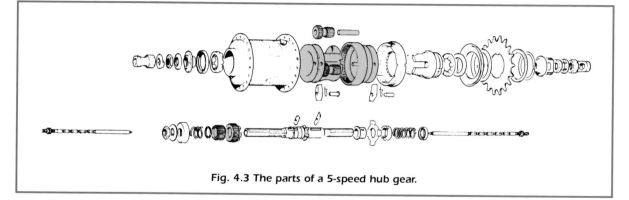

Fig. 4.3 The parts of a 5-speed hub gear.

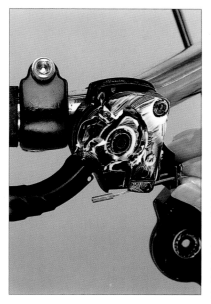

Above: This is how the 5-speed's two cables enter the single-lever shifter.

Below: Detail photo of Shimano 7-speed hub gear. It is adjusted by lining up color-coded markings on the mechanism while the 4th gear is selected.

6. Check whether this gear engages properly.

7. If the first gear does not engage properly, return to the fourth gear and tighten the looser cables one notch, repeating steps 5–7 as necessary until the first gear works properly.

8. Check all the gears in turn, and readjust, if necessary.

Replace Shifter or Cable

This has to be done if the problem cannot be solved by means of adjustment and lubrication. If the cause is clearly not here either, the hub gear mechanism itself is at fault. If you are faced with this predicament, it will be easier to replace the entire wheel complete with hub. You can then take your time disassembling the old hub to see whether you can find an obviously defective part.

Each shifter is basically designed for the same manufacturer's hub. However, there are adaptor pieces that allow the use of one manufacturer's cable with another manufacturer's adjusting mechanism. In the case of the 3-speed, it is often possible to use non-matching shifters. Five-speeds can be operated with two separate 3-speed shifters of any make instead of the original complicated 5-position shifter. For the following procedures, you'll need a screwdriver and a crescent wrench.

Removal Procedure:

1. Loosen the cable adjuster at the hub.

2. Pull the cable back toward the shifter for enough slack.

3. Pull the shift lever in as far as possible (or, in the case of a 5-speed, open it up to gain access) and remove the nipple from the recess in the shifter. Then hold the cable and push the lever up into the high position.

4. Pull the cable back out of the shifter and off the guides and stops.

5. Remove the part that has to be replaced (cable or shifter).

Installation Procedure:

1. When replacing the lever, install it in the right location.

2. Pull the shift lever in as far as possible or, in the case of a 5-speed lever, open it up to gain access. Feed the nipple in and hook it in the recess in the shifter.

3. Hold the cable pulled taut and place it over the various guides and stops.

4. At the hub, attach it to the control chain or the bell crank.

5. Adjust the gears as described above.

Above: Shimano 7-speed hub, showing the controls and the adjustment mechanism.

Below: Fine-tune the Shimano 7-speed shifter by adjusting the control cable tension. LIke some newer derailleur shifters, this shift lever is equipped with an indicator to show which gear is selected.

Adjust Hub Gear Bearings

The gear hub's ball bearings must be maintained just like those of other hubs. The adjustment procedure is quite easy if you have the manufacturer's special wrench which is usually supplied with the bike or the hub. Basically it's a regular adjustable cup-and-cone ball bearing, but it has a special locknut. Any adjustments are done on the LH side.

Procedure:

1. Loosen the LH axle nut 2–3 turns to the left.

2. Loosen the locknut 1–2 turns.

3. Tighten the adjusting nut for the cone fully, then back it off to the left by a quarter turn.

4. Hold the adjusting nut in this position and tighten the locknut.

5. Tighten the axle nut, while keeping the wheel centrally positioned.

6. Check the bearing to make sure it is neither too loose nor too tight, and readjust if necessary.

7-Speed Hubs

Gear hubs with 7 speeds and a built-in back-pedaling brake are made by both Sachs and Shimano. The general maintenance instructions correspond closely to those for 5-speed models. The controls for the Sachs unit are contained in the "click box," a plastic housing on the outside of the hub, and any adjusting is done there. This box can simply be unhooked if the wheel has to be removed. The Shimano model's mechanism is contained in a narrow disk between the chain and the RH drop-out, requiring the removal of the cables from the adjustment mechanism—and subsequent readjustment of the gears —if the wheel has to be removed.

Adjusting Procedure:

1. Make sure the cable is not pinched or damaged.

2. Select the first gear and turn the cranks one turn.

3. On Sachs hubs, pull the click box off the pin protruding from the axle, then push it back on until the cable is taut.

4. On Shimano models, turn in the adjuster until the cable is taut.

5. Shift into each of the other gears and return to the first gear, then fine-tune the adjustment.

Note:
The Shimano control mechanism, being open to the elements, tends to malfunction if it gets wet and dirty, especially at low temeratures. Regularly clean and lubricate the mechanism by the side of the hub to prevent these problems.

CHAPTER 5

The Brakes

Modern sidepull brake as used on most road bikes—and most suitable for bikes with narrow tires.

BICYCLE brakes come in two major types—rim brakes and hub brakes—but the former are by far the more common. Even among rim brakes, there are two distinct types, namely calliper and stirrup brakes. The vast majority of modern bikes come with some kind of cable-operated calliper brakes, while the rod-operated stirrup brakes are now quite rare. The coaster brake is sometimes found on children's bikes and cruisers. The drum brake is used on tandems as an auxiliary brake, as is the disk brake, which is also used on a few high-tech mountain bikes.

On all rim brakes, two brake pads are pushed against the rim. Among calliper brakes, sidepull and centerpull brakes are used on road bikes and installed as complete units. Cantilever brakes and cam-operated models are used on mountain bikes, hybrids and some touring bikes. They consist of individual brake arms that are mounted on bosses which are brazed, welded or bonded on the front fork at the front and either the chain stays or the seat stays at the rear. At the rear, cantilever brakes are always installed on the seat stays, whereas other mountain bike brakes are sometimes mounted underneath the chain stays. For mountain bikes, there is also a centerpull type, called a U-brake, with individual brake arms mounted on pivot bosses mounted on the frame or the front fork.

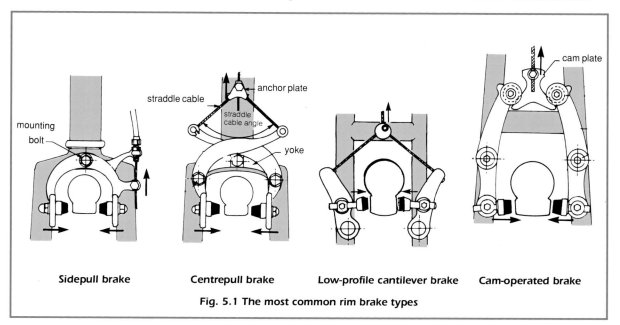

| Sidepull brake | Centrepull brake | Low-profile cantilever brake | Cam-operated brake |

Fig. 5.1 The most common rim brake types

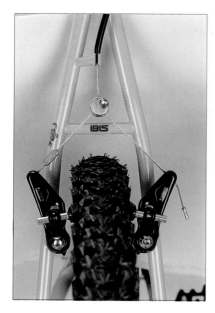

Above: Typical cantilever brake as used on most mountain bikes, as well as on hybrids and touring bikes. Note the angle between the two halves of the straddle cable that connects the two brake arms.

Below: Centerpull brake. Although these are not used very much any more on modern bikes, they are perhaps the most trouble-free brakes on the market.

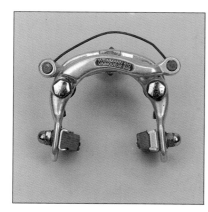

In addition to the types shown, there are several special models available, usually intended for mountain bike use, including hydraulically operated calliper brakes and hub-mounted disc brakes.

All of the common brakes are connected to the hand lever by means of a flexible Bowden cable. Usually, the LH lever controls the front brake, while the RH lever operates the rear brake, although they can be reversed according to your preference.

On many mountain bikes, the cable for the front brake runs either over a roller mounted under the handlebar stem or through a hole in the stem. Both solutions are a bit of a pain, since they require a full brake readjustment whenever the handlebar position has been changed. It is better to install an anchor that is clamped between the lock washer and the locknut of the headset.

Cantilever and centerpull brakes have a connecting cable between the two brake arms. This cable must be kept as short as possible (top angle of cable triangle as big as possible) if the two sides are to be pushed together enough for adequate brake force. Today's low-profile cantilever brakes differ from the older versions in that they do not protrude as far as conventional models. Shimano's versions don't have a conventional straddle cable: instead, the main cable runs to one of the brake arms and the second brake arm is connected to it via a short cable and a connecting clamp.

Brake Maintenance

From a maintenance standpoint, the brakes should be considered as complete systems, each incorporating levers, control cables and various pieces of mounting hardware, as well as the brake itself. In fact, brake problems are most often due to inadequacies of some component in the control system. Consequently, it will be necessary to approach the problem systematically, trying to isolate the fault by checking off one component after the other.

When the brakes work inconsistently, often with associated vibrations or squealing, the cause is usually found either in dirt and grease on the rims, loosely mounted fittings, or incorrect brake pad positioning. First check the condition of the rims, then the attachments of brake pads, brake arms, brake units, cables, anchors and levers. If the rim is dented, there is usually no other solution than to replace it, while all other causes can usually be eliminated quite easily.

Adjust Brake Pads

This simple job is often not only the solution to squealing, rumbling or vibrating noises, but may also solve inadequate braking performance and prevent serious mishaps. As the brake pad wears, its position relative to the rim changes. On a cantilever brake, it moves radially inward—farther away from the tire and toward the spokes— while it moves up toward the tires on all other brakes. If left

Above: Hold the brake pad firmly in place on the rim while adjusting and tightening its mounting bolt.

Below: To test the brake, pull in the lever as far as you can—the brake should stop the bike when there is a 2 cm (¾ in.) clearance between the lever and the handlebars.

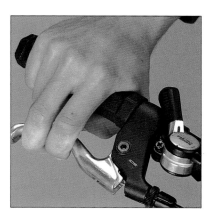

unchecked, chances are it will eventually hit the spokes or the tire instead of the rim.

To prevent this, it is not enough to follow the systematic brake test described below regularly: you also have to check the position of the brake pads as they contact the rim, and readjust them if they don't align. In addition, it is preferable if the front end of the brake pad is about 1–2 mm closer to the rim than the rear. This is to compensate for the deformation of the brake arm as brake force is applied, which tends to twist the back of the brake pad in. Only when you adjust them this way, referred to as *toed in*, will the brake force be equally distributed over the entire length of the brake pad.

Tools and equipment: 5 mm Allen wrench
pliers   9 mm wrench

Procedure:

1. Loosen the nut or bolt that holds the brake pad to the brake arm by about one turn.

2. While applying the corresponding brake lever with modest hand force, move the brake pads into the position illustrated, then increase lever force. You may have to twist the brake pad and the underlying spherical and cupped washers—or whatever other device is provided for angular adjustment—to achieve this position.

3. Place a small piece of cardboard, about 1 mm (¹⁄₃₂–¹⁄₁₆ in.) thick between the brake pad and the rim, over the back 12 mm (½ in.) of the brake pad.

4. Tighten the bolt fully, while holding the brake pad against the side of the rim firmly with the pliers to make sure it does not shift from its correct position.

5. Check to make sure the brake works correctly, and fine-tune the adjustment if necessary.

Brake Test

In order to verify their condition and effectiveness, test the brakes according to the following systematic procedure at regular intervals —about once a month under normal conditions. The idea is to establish whether the deceleration achieved with each brake is as high as the physical constraints of the bicycle's geometry will allow. Tools are not needed for this test.

Procedure:

1. Ride the bike at a brisk walking speed (about 8 km/h, or 5 mph) on a straight, level surface without traffic.

Above: On mountain bikes and other machines with flat handlebars, the cable can be lifted out of the lever when the slots in the lever housing, the barrel adjuster, and the locknut are lined up—after the cable tension is released.

Below: Typical modern lever for bikes with drop handlebars. On these models, there is no adjuster on the lever but at the brake itself.

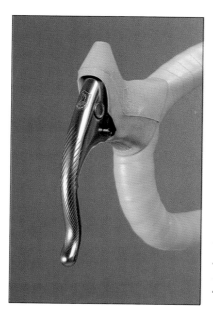

2. Apply the rear brake hard. If the rear wheel skids, you have all the braking you can use in the rear—a deceleration of 3.5 m/sec^2.

3. Repeat the procedure with the front brake. But be careful—you don't want to go over the handlebars. If the rear wheel starts to lift off, a deceleration of 6.5 m/sec^2 has been reached, and that's as much as you'll ever want. Let go of the front brake again.

Brake System Inspection

If one brake or the other fails the test described above, check the entire brake system and adjust or correct as necessary. Usually, no tools are needed for this inspection, but you may have to use a variety of items to solve individual problems uncovered this way.

Procedure:

1. Check to make sure the rim and the brake pads are clean. The presence of wet or greasy dirt plays havoc with their operation. Wipe clean or degrease the rim and scrape the brake pad with steel wool.

2. Check whether the cables move freely and are not pinched or damaged. In the case of special controls, such as hydraulics or pull rods, check them for correct operation and installation. Clean, free and lubricate or replace cables that don't move freely. Repair or replace anything else found wanting.

3. Inspect the levers—they must be firmly installed and there must be at least 2 cm (¾ in.) clearance between lever and handlebars when the brake is applied fully. If necessary, tighten, lubricate, adjust.

4. Make sure the brake arms themselves are free to move without resistance, and that they are returned to clear the wheel fully by the spring tension when the lever is released. If necessary, loosen, adjust, lubricate, overhaul or replace.

Adjust Brake

Roughly the same operation is followed for all types of calliper brakes, although the adjustment mechanisms may be installed in different locations. Regarding tools, it is handy to have a pair of needle-nose pliers to adjust a centerpull brake, while you may need an Allen wrench or a wrench to fit the cable clamping nut on all models.

The most common type of brake adjustment is that required to tighten the cable a little in order to compensate for brake pad wear. This operation is about the same, whatever type of brake you have.

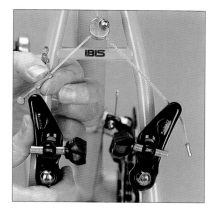

On cantilever and centerpull brakes, the straddle cable, or connecting cable, is attached to the brake cable via an anchor plate. It can be lifted out on one side to release the brake.

First carry out the brake pad adjustment mentioned above. If you don't, there is a risk of the brake pad sooner or later slipping off the side of the rim, hitting either the tire or the spokes.

Tools and Equipment:
5 mm Allen wrench

9 mm wrench
pliers

Procedure:

1. If the brake does not perform adequately, the cable tension has to be increased. Do that initially by tightening the cable adjuster by 2 turns.

2. Verify whether the brake now engages fully when 2 cm (¾ in.) clearance remains between lever and handlebars.

3. If the correct adjustment cannot be achieved within the adjusting range of the cable adjuster, first screw it in all the way, then loosen the cable clamping bolt, pull the cable further and tighten the clamping bolt again. On the centerpull brake this can be done by wrapping the cable around the needle nose pliers and twisting it further. Now fine-tune with the adjuster.

4. If after all this adjusting the brake finally transmits enough tension but does not clear the rim adequately when disengaged, you will have to check all parts of the system and replace or overhaul as necessary.

Adjust Roller-Cam Brake

This particular type of brake has some peculiar features that make it extremely effective for touring bikes and mountain bikes—providing it is adjusted correctly. The adjustment procedure is quite different from that for other brakes. Carry out this procedure whenever the brake does not seem to be operating properly. Before making any changes, make sure the rim is clean; sometimes it is merely a matter of a greasy and slippery rim.

Tools and equipment:
5 mm Allen wrench

9–10 mm wrench
14 mm cone wrench

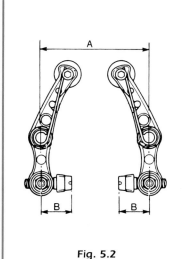

Fig. 5.2
Roller-cam brake dimensions

Procedure:

1. Check the alignment of the brake pads on the rim: they must lie flat and fully contact the side of the rim when the lever is pulled hard.

2. Check whether the brake pads protrude the correct distance from the brake arm. Measure the distance between the mounting pivots and determine the correct protrusion (Fig. 5.2) from the following table:

Dimension A	Dimension B
92 mm	29 mm
90 mm	28 mm
88 mm	27 mm
86 mm	26 mm
84 mm	25 mm

Above: Adjusting a sidepull brake, using a universal brake centering tool. Most high-end sidepull brakes have their own centering device.

Below: Shimano STI brakes can be centered by means of the centering worm screw in one of the brake arms.

If the dimensions do not match, adjust until they do.

3. Check the centering of the brake pads. First make sure the rim itself is centered between the frame stays (or fork blades, if the brake is used in the front) and correct if necessary. If the distance between the side of the rim and the brake pad is different on each side, adjust.

4. The centering of the brake is a function of the spring tension, and most models have two separate springs that can be adjusted individually. To do this, first check to make sure the fixing nuts on the brake arm pivot bolts are tight, then use a 14 mm cone wrench (or any flat open-ended wrench of this size) to turn the pivot bushings immediately under the brake arms by only a very slight angular amount, until the two brake arms are centered relative to the rim.

5. Sometimes it is necessary to readjust the brake pad location, following points 3–4 above, after this operation, so that the brake pads are the same distance and touch the rim correctly.

Centering Rim Brakes

One of the most frustrating problems can be the off-centered position of a brake, causing it to rub along the rim on one side while clearing it on the other. If the problem is intermittent, first try to alleviate it by truing the wheel (see Chapter 7). If the problem is constant, the solution will be different depending on the kind of brake you have.

Centerpull Brake:

On this type of brake, it is generally a simple matter of twisting the yoke on which the brake arms are installed.

1. First make sure the brake is firmly attached. Tighten the mounting bolt if necessary, while depressing the lever and holding the brake centered.

2. If the brake is properly fastened and still off-set, take a big screwdriver and a hammer. Place the screwdriver on the pivot point that is too high and lightly tap it with the hammer.

3. Repeat or correct until the brake is centered.

Sidepull Brake:

Here the problem is due to the stubbornness of the mounting bolt, if it twists back into an off-center position. Straightening is easier said than done: it will find its way back to this wrong position the next time the brake is applied. Some brake models come with a special adjusting tool with which the mounting bolt is repositioned,

Above: Most modern cantilever brakes are centered with a little adjuster screw in one of the brake arms.

Below: The cantilever brake arms can be removed by unscrewing the pivot bolt.

each of them with its own instructions. There is also a universal tool, which may work on brakes without their own special tool: place each of the pins inside a loop of the spring and twist in the appropriate direction. On other models, for which no tool is provided, proceed as follows:

Tools and equipment:
2 mm Allen wrench

13–14 mm cone wrench
6 mm Allen wrench

Procedure:

1. If the mounting bolt has flats between the brake and the fork or the frame, place the cone wrench on these flats and the second wrench or Allen wrench on the nut at the end of the mounting bolt. If not, put a wrench on each end of the mounting bolt.

2. Older brakes may have two nuts on the top of the mounting bolt—the outside nut if you have to turn clockwise, the inside one to turn counterclockwise.

3. To twist the mounting bolt, turn both tools simultaneously.

If after all this the problem remains or returns, install a flat, thin steel washer between the brake body and the fork or rear stay bridge (or the shaped spacer installed there). This will provide a smooth "unbiased" surface that can be twisted into the desired position, rather than getting stuck in existing incorrect indentations.

Cantilever Brake:

1. Most models have a 2 mm hexagonal recess in one of the pivots that is turned one way or the other, to tension a spring that is hidden inside the bushing.

2. Other models have 14 mm flats between the pivot boss and the brake arms, which can be adjusted by turning the pivot bolt with a matching cone wrench.

3. On most Dia-Compe brakes, loosen the pivot bolt and turn the bushing behind it with a 13 mm cone wrench, and tighten the bolt again.

4. On older versions without a centering screw, bend one of the springs that spread the brake levers in or out a little, using needle-nose pliers.

U-Brake:

This kind of brake usually has a small adjusting screw in one of the brake arms that is loosened to bring that arm in, or tightened to bring the other one in. If this does not solve the problem, disassemble the brake and bend the spring in or out until it is symmetrical.

Above: Most modern sidepull brakes have a quick-release lever to tension or slacken the cable so it can be adjusted more easily. It is also used to open up the brake arms far enough to slide the wheel in or out.

Below: View of the inside of a cantilever brake pivot. The return spring sits in the cylindrical bushing between the boss and the brake arm.

Roller-Cam Brake:

This is the most popular form of what I referred to as a cam-operated brake. This brake usually comes with a similar little adjusting screw on one of the brake arms that is tightened or loosened to center the brake arms.

Overhaul or Replace Brake

This work is recommended once a year—more often if the bike is used a lot in inclement weather, or whenever the brake gives unsatisfactory performance and adjustment does not solve the problem.

Although there are slight differences in the procedure as it applies to different brakes, you will find a general description here, including comments for specific models. Most comments apply to all brakes, though.

This work is most easily carried out while the wheel is removed. For easy wheel removal on brakes without quick-release, push the brake pads together just enough to unhook the cable (centerpull, U-brake or cantilever). On the roller-cam, remove the cam plate, then loosen the tip of one spring and spread the brake arms asymmetrically.

Tools and equipment:
13–14 mm cone wrench

5 mm Allen wrench
needle-nose pliers

Removal Procedure:

1. Pull the brake arms together at the brake pads and release the cable—on the roller cam-brake by twisting the cam plate out from between the rollers.

2. Check condition of the cable and replace if necessary: remove the cable anchor clamp using a wrench on the nut and an Allen wrench on the bolt part. Pull the cable out, and later insert the new one. If an end cap is installed on the end of the cable, it must be pulled off with needle-nose pliers—I recommend soldering or crimping the end of the cable to prevent fraying, following the instructions under *Replace Brake Cable* on page 57.

3. Unscrew the fixing nut on top of the brake arm pivot bolt of each brake arm. In the case of a sidepull or centerpull brake, remove the whole unit.

4. Using the needle-nose pliers, remove the upper end of the spring of each brake arm from its seating, then pull the brake arm, the spring and the bushing off the pivot stud.

5. Clean, inspect and, if necessary, repair or replace any damaged parts. In particular, remove any rust from the pivot stud of the pivot boss, then apply some bearing grease to this location. On the roller-cam, you may remove the rollers from the brake arms, and install these

Above: Sidepull and centerpull brakes are removed and installed with a single mounting bolt accessible from the front of the brake mounting bridge (in the rear) or the back of the fork crown (in the front).

Below: Many brake pads form an integral unit that eliminates the need for a separate metal holder. They are held with a bolt that screws directly into an internally screwed boss embedded in the brake pad material.

again after inspection, cleaning and lubrication.

6. If appropriate, remove the brake pads and their fixing bolts, in order to clean and, if necessary, replace them (if the brake pads are badly worn).

Installation Procedure:

1. Ascertain that all parts are functional, clean and lightly greased.

2. Put the springs on the pivot studs, with the long arms of the spring pointing up and to the inside.

3. Install the adjusting bushing over the top of the spring around the stud of each mounting boss, the cylindrical bushing part protruding.

4. Install the brake arms on the adjusting bushings, followed by the washer and the nut or the bolt.

5. In the case of a roller-cam brake, hook the end of the spring into its seating at the end of the roller pin of each brake arm.

6. Push the brake pads together and reinstall the cam plate between the rollers (on the roller-cam) or the connecting cable (on other models).

7. If appropriate, readjust the cable tension by adjusting at the brake lever or by clamping the anchor plate (U-brake or cantilever brake) or the cam plate (roller-cam brake) at a different point on the cable.

8. In the case of sidepull or centerpull brakes, re-install the complete unit.

9. Adjust the brakes.

Adjust Brake Lever

Although there are a number of different makes and models within the categories of road and mountain bike brake levers, the similarities are generally so great that the following general description covers all but the most unusual models. All are designed to fit standard 22.2 mm (⅞ in.) diameter handlebars as used on all regular mountain bikes. Any bike with a different diameter handlebar also requires a modified or custom-built clamp for the brake lever.

The brake lever must be installed so that it can be easily reached and pulled in so far that the brake is fully applied when a gap of about 20 mm (¾ in.) remains between the brake lever and the handlebars at the tightest point. There are four forms of adjustment that apply to the brake lever:

☐ mounting location   ☐ cable routing
☐ reach   ☐ cable tension

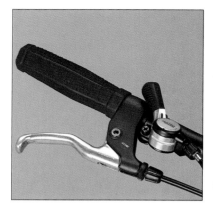

Above: On most mountain bikes, the brake cable adjuster is integrated with the brake lever.

Below: On some models, the reach can be adjusted by means of a simple screw in the side of the lever mount.

Tools and equipment:
5 mm Allen wrench
9–10 mm wrench

small screwdriver (for older models)

Procedure—Position Adjustment:

1. Determine in which direction the brake lever should be moved or rotated to provide adequate and comfortable operation.

2. If necessary, move any other parts installed on the handlebars (e.g. shift levers) in order to allow moving the brake lever to the desired location.

3. Loosen the bolt that clamps the lever to the handlebars by one or two turns, then twist or slide the lever to its desired location and tighten the bolt again.

4. Make sure the lever does not extend beyond the end of the handlebars. You want to avoid accidental brake application while passing closely by any objects in your path behind which the brake levers might get caught.

5. Most road bikes have an internal bolt that can be reached once the lever is pulled, preferably after removing the cable. On old models it requires a screwdriver, while more recent versions require the use of a 5 mm Allen wrench. Make sure not to unscrew this bolt all the way, because it will be hard to reinstall.

6. Retighten any other components that may have been moved to new locations. Make sure all parts are in their most convenient location and are properly tightened.

Procedure—Reach Adjustment:

1. Most (though not all) mountain bike brake levers are equipped with a set-screw that can be turned in or out in order to limit the range of travel of the brake lever as appropriate to the reach of your hand.

2. Check the distance between the handlebars and the brake lever in unapplied position compared with the maximum comfortable reach of your hand. In general, it should be opened as far as possible commensurate with the size of your hand, since a larger reach allows the most effective brake application and the most accurate adjustment of the brake cable.

3. If adjustment is necessary, tighten the range-adjusting screw to reduce the range (i.e., the maximum opening position), or loosen it to increase the range.

4. Check to make sure the brake can be applied properly, and adjust the brake cable, following the

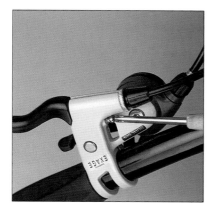

Above: Another form of reach adjustment by means of a screw in the back of the lever mount.

Below: To loosen or tighten a brake lever for use with drop handlebars, you gain access to the mounting bolt by pulling the lever in all the way. You may have to undo the cable at the brake first.

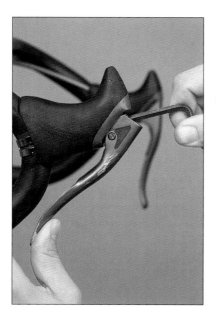

appropriate instructions below, if necessary.

Adjust Brake Cable

The main brake adjustment—the only one usually required from time to time to compensate for brake pad wear—is that of the brake cable. To adjust the brake cable tension, either the lever or the brake unit is equipped with a barrel adjuster. In case the adjusting range of this device is not adequate, the attachment of the cable to the brake itself can be changed. The latter adjustment depends on the type of brake used, but the instructions can be generalized enough to cover most situations.

Tools and equipment:
needle-nose pliers

5 mm Allen wrench or 9 mm wrench

Procedure:

1. If the brake does not apply adequate force when the lever is pulled, the cable must be tightened. If, on the other hand, the brake seems to be applied too soon—if the brake scrapes the side of the rim when the lever is not pulled—it should be slackened a little.

2. To tighten the brake cable, hold the locknut and screw the barrel adjuster out by several turns. Then hold the barrel adjuster in place while screwing in the locknut.

3. To release the brake cable, hold the barrel adjuster and back off the locknut by several turns, then screw the barrel adjuster in further, and finally tighten the locknut, while holding the barrel adjuster to stop it from turning.

4. Check and readjust, if necessary, until operation of the brake is optimal.

5. If the adjusting range of the barrel adjuster is not adequate, screw it in all the way, after having backed off the locknut fully. Then proceed to adjust the clamping location of the cable at the brake.

6. The end of the cable at the brake unit itself is clamped onto an anchor by means of either an eye bolt or a pinch plate held under a bolt-and-nut combination. Loosen the nut of this unit and pull the cable through a little further, then clamp it in properly at the new location by tightening the nut while holding the bolt.

7. Check once more and adjust the barrel adjuster at the brake lever if necessary.

Above: Exposing the end of the brake cable on a Shimano STI brake lever.

Below:
Left: Attaching the brake cable and the straddle cable on a cantilever or centerpull brake.

Center: This is how a U-brake is centered.

Right: The brake cables on mountain bikes are routed through split cable guides that act as stops for the cable casings.

Straddle Cables

Sometimes cantilever brakes don't work properly because the angle between the two halves of the straddle cable is too sharp. Keeping the straddle cable clamped in as short as possible while still clearing the tire will improve its performance.

On some models, the main cable ends in a triangular anchor plate over which a separate straddle cable runs. On other models, mainly by Shimano, the main cable runs through a round anchor plate to one brake arm, and the other brake arm is connected to the anchor plate by a single short cable. In the latter case, you can loosen the screw holding the main cable to the anchor plate and clamp it closer in, making sure the two cable ends run symmetrically. Markings on the round anchor plate show how the cables should run.

Replace Brake Cable

This should be done about once a year—or whenever it is pinched, corroded or otherwise damaged, especially if signs of broken strands are in evidence. Make sure you get a model that has the same kind of nipple (visible inside the lever) as the old one.

Tools and equipment:
5 mm Allen wrench or 9 mm wrench
cable cutters
grease
soldering equipment or crimping tool

Removal Procedure:

1. Release tension on the brake by squeezing the brake arms against the rim, then unhook the connecting cable (U-brake or cantilever brake) or the cam plate (roller-cam brake).

2. Unscrew the eye bolt or clamp nut that holds the cable to the connecting plate, the cam plate or the brake itself (depending on the type of brake), making sure not to lose the various parts.

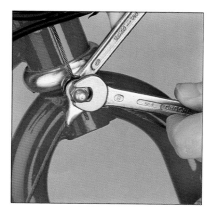

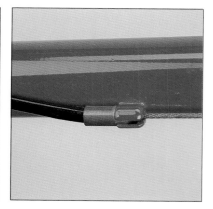

Top: Cut the end of the brake cable with cable cutters to avoid fraying.

Center: Pull the cable taut before tightening the cable clamp bolt.

Bottom: If you don't solder the strands of the inner cable together (before cutting it to size at that point), at least crimp a cable end cap on it to prevent fraying.

3. Push the cable through toward the lever, then pull it out once enough slack is generated, catching any pieces of cable casing and end pieces.

4. Screw the adjuster and the locknut at the lever in and leave them in such a position that their slots are aligned with the slot in the lever housing, so the cable can be lifted out.

5. Remove the cable, dislodging the nipple from the lever.

Installation Procedure:

1. Establish whether the cable casing is still intact and replace it if necessary, cutting it to length in such a way that no hook is formed at the end (bending the metal of the spiral back if necessary).

2. Lubricate the cable with grease.

3. Place the nipple in the lever and guide the cable through the slot in the lever, the various guides and stops, and the sections of casing.

4. Attach the end in the eye bolt or clamp nut at the brake.

5. Adjust the cable tension as described above.

6. If you have the equipment to do it, solder the strands of the cable together at the end to prevent fraying, before you cut it off.

7. Cut off the excess cable length, leaving about 2.5–3 cm (1–1¼ in.) projecting. This is best done with a special cable cutting tool, though it can be done with other sharp and strong pliers, such as diagonal cutters.

8. If you have not soldered the end of the cable, put a crimp on the end.

Coaster Brake Maintenance

Especially on children's bikes, coaster brakes are still in use. In fact today's models can be quite effective. Since there is no hand lever and cable or rod mechanism, maintenance is quite simple. The major maintenance described here will be adjustment of the wheel bearings and other bearing work. These brakes tend to run hot when used vigorously over longer distances. In extreme cases, the lubricant burns out of the bearings. If this happens, partly dismantle the bearings—after the hub has cooled—and repack them, using the manufacturer's recommended special high-temperature grease.

Adjust Coaster Brake Hub Bearings

From time to time, check the bearings as described for the regular hub. If they are too loose or tight, adjust them without removing the wheel from the bike. The special wrench needed is usually supplied with the bike or the brake hub—if not, you can order it through a bike shop).

Above: On all hub brakes, whether coaster brake, drum brake or disc brake, the brake plate has a counter-lever that is attached to a fixed part of the bike to counter the braking force.

Procedure:

1. Loosen the LH axle nut 2–3 turns.

2. Loosen the round locknut with recesses about one turn.

3. If the hub is equipped with a square end on the RH axle end, turn it clockwise to loosen the axle, counterclockwise to tighten it.

4. On models without a square axle end, remove the locknut altogether and loosen the underlying shaped plate that engages the cone: to the left to loosen, to the right to tighten the bearing.

5. Tighten first the locknut, restraining the axle or the shaped plate; then tighten the axle nut.

Drum Brake Maintenance

These brakes are sometimes used on tandems and in some countries on touring and utility bikes. Maintenance operations include adjustment of the cable (or the control rod on models so operated) and the bearing. Very rarely, you may have to exchange the brake segments, or shoes, when the liners are worn or contaminated. In the latter case, dismantle the brake and remove the old shoes which can be relined or exchanged by a motorcycle brake specialist.

Adjust Drum Brake

Essentially, this is done as on any other hand-operated brake. The cable adjuster is used to increase the cable tension if the brake does not engage properly, and is loosened if it does not clear when the lever is released. As with the rim brake, the cable, the lever, the guides and the anchors must be checked, and if necessary cleaned, freed, lubricated or replaced when adjustment does not have the desired effect.

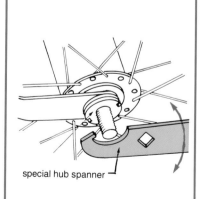

special hub spanner

Fig. 5.3
On hub brakes without sealed bearings, the bearings can be adjusted with the manufacturer's special tool.

Adjust Drum Brake Hub Bearings

The need for this is established as described in Chapter 7 for the regular hub. All you need is a 15 or 16 mm wrench and the special wrench that may be available for the particular model. The wheel may be left on the bike.

Procedure:

1. Loosen the axle nut on the control side by 3–4 turns.

2. Loosen the locknut by 1–2 turns, and lift the lock washer.

3. The adjusting plate, which engages the bearing cone, can now be turned to the right to tighten the bearings, or to the left to loosen them. Do not overtighten.

Above: Adjustment of a typical drum brake with cable operation.

Below: The brake drum can be dismantled, revealing the brake mechanism and the brake shoes.

4. Hold the adjusting plate while tightening the locknut.

5. Tighten the axle nut, making sure the wheel is properly centered.

6. Check and repeat the adjustment if necessary.

Overhaul Drum Brake

This can become necessary when the bearings or the brake pads are so worn or damaged that adjusting does not solve the problem. The wheel must be removed from the bike. Disengage the control cable and remove the bolt that holds the brake plate, or torque arm, to the fork or the chain stay.

Dismantling Procedure:

1. Loosen the locknut completely and remove the lock washer.

2. Loosen the cone by means of the adjusting plate (or, after removing the latter, by means of a wrench), and remove it.

3. Remove the brake plate on which the entire mechanism is installed, while catching the bearing balls, which are usually contained in a retainer.

Maintenance and Assembly Procedure:

1. Clean and inspect all components:

☐ Replace the brake shoes if the pads are worn down to less than 3 mm (1/8 in.) at any point or when they are contaminated with oil and simply roughing them with steel wool does not restore them.

☐ Replace the bearings balls with their retainer and any other bearing components that are damaged (pitted, grooved, corroded).

2. Fill the bearing cups with bearing grease and push the bearing balls into the cups.

3. Apply just a little grease to the pivot and the cam on which the brake shoes sit.

4. Wipe excess grease away to make sure it cannot reach the brake liners or brake drum.

5. Install the brake plate with the brake shoes mounted on it.

6. Screw the cone in and tighten it with the aid of the adjusting plate.

7. Install the lock washer and the locknut, while holding the adjusting plate so it does not turn.

8. Check the bearings and adjust as necessary.

9. After installation of the wheel, check operation of the brake and adjust the cable tension, if necessary.

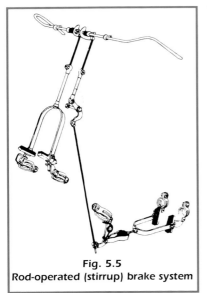

Fig. 5.5
Rod-operated (stirrup) brake system

Stirrup and Other Rod-Operated Brakes

Stirrup brakes are still used on some traditional English bikes, as well as in much of the Third World. They are not operated by cables but by means of pull rods that connect the lever via a series of frame-mounted pivots to the brake arms, which are pulled radially in toward the inside of the rim. In some other parts of the world, you may find drum brakes operated the same way.

Stirrup brakes and other rod-operated brakes are usually adjusted by means of a knurled round nut or a screw at the end of the rod where it is attached to the stirrup or the drum brake's activating lever. Apart from the usual brake shoe maintenance, they should be lubricated at the pivot points once a month; at the same time each of the attachment nuts should be tightened. Straighten any bent rods and your rod-operated brakes will work forever.

CHAPTER 6

The Drivetrain

THE bicycle's drivetrain comprises the parts that transmit the rider's legwork to the rear wheel. They are the bottom bracket with cranks and chainrings, the pedals, the chain, and the freewheel with cogs. The derailleurs, which are sometimes considered part of the drivetrain, are covered separately in Chapter 4, which is devoted to the gearing system.

The Cranks

Virtually all modern bicycles are equipped with aluminum cotterless cranks. These are held onto the square tapered ends of the bottom bracket spindle by a matching square tapered hole and a bolt or nut, depending on the design of the spindle. Since the variety held with bolts is usually of higher quality than that held with nuts, choose the former when replacing the bottom bracket.

The bolt or nut is covered by a dustcap, which protects the screw thread in the recess. The screw thread is used to pull the crank off the spindle for maintenance or replacement. The RH crank has an attachment "spider," to which the chainrings are bolted.

The tool used to remove a crank, the crank extractor, consists of two parts, which may be permanently combined: a wrench for the crank bolt or nut and the actual extractor. Crank bolts and nuts come in sizes 14–16 mm; most quality bikes use 15 mm crank bolts, cheaper models use 14 mm, while at least one manufacturer, TA, uses 16mm.

Above: The crankset is the center of the bicycle's drivetrain. This Campagnolo Chorus is typical of the kind of cranksets used on high-quality racing bikes.

Below: The crank is held onto the spindle by means of a bolt that clamps it onto the spindle's square tapered end.

Right: The components of the drivetrain on a 16-speed derailleur bike.

This page:
Above: Check the bottom bracket
and the cranks.
Below: To remove the crank, first
loosen the crank bolt.

Facing page:
Top: Use the crank extractor to pull
the crank off.
Bottom: The crank's square hole
matches the spindle end.

The crank extractor fits into the threaded hole surrounding the crank bolt, and pulls the crank off its spindle when tightened with the wrench. For the 22 mm threaded holes found on most bikes, I prefer the Campagnolo tool, which has a separate long-handled wrench. TA cranks have 23 mm threaded holes that require a matching tool.

Some Campagnolo and older Shimano cranksets do not use a conventional crank bolt, but a one-key release system. These require only one Allen wrench (6 mm for Shimano and 7 mm for Campagnolo) to both loosen the crank and pull it off the spindle. Whatever you do, don't attempt to remove the insert from the crank. If it becomes loose, you must take it out, clean the screw thread, and cement it in place with an anaerobic locking adhesive, such as Loctite Blue.

A new bike's cranks should be tightened every 40 km (25 miles) for the first 200 km (125 miles), since initially the soft aluminum of the cranks deforms so much that the connection between the spindle and the crank tends to come loose. This is the reason you should carry the crank bolt wrench in your repair kit. Beyond that, the crank is merely removed when it is damaged or when you have to adjust or overhaul the bottom bracket.

It is not uncommon in off-road cycling to bend a crank during a fall. Before you replace the entire crank, let a bike mechanic try to straighten it out. This requires a special tool that is not worth buying for the average home mechanic.

Replace Crank

This job is necessary when a crank or an entire crankset has to be replaced. It also has to be done for many maintenance jobs on the bottom bracket.

Tools and equipment:

4–7 mm Allen wrench	crank bolt wrench
adjustable pin wrench	cloth
crank extractor	grease

Removal Procedure:

1. Remove the dustcap, which can generally be done with a coin, though some models require the use of an Allen wrench or adjustable pin wrench. Some recent Shimano versions have Allen crank bolts with a flexible grommet, eliminating the need for a separate dustcap.

2. Unscrew the bolt or the nut with the wrench part of the crank tool, while holding the crank firmly.

3. Remove the washer that lies under the bolt or nut. This is an important step; if you forget to do this, you will not be able to remove the crank, but will damage it.

4. Make sure the internal part of the crank extractor is retracted as far as it will go.

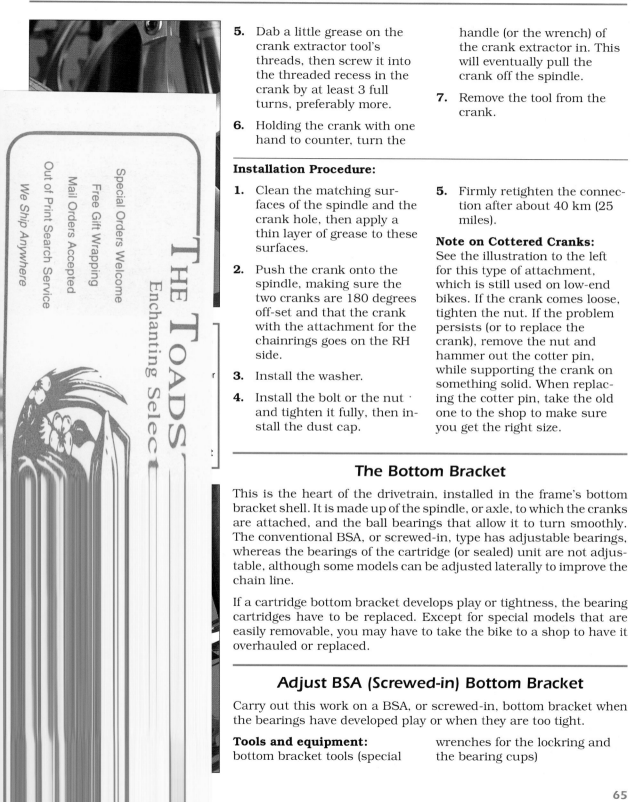

5. Dab a little grease on the crank extractor tool's threads, then screw it into the threaded recess in the crank by at least 3 full turns, preferably more.

6. Holding the crank with one hand to counter, turn the handle (or the wrench) of the crank extractor in. This will eventually pull the crank off the spindle.

7. Remove the tool from the crank.

Installation Procedure:

1. Clean the matching surfaces of the spindle and the crank hole, then apply a thin layer of grease to these surfaces.

2. Push the crank onto the spindle, making sure the two cranks are 180 degrees off-set and that the crank with the attachment for the chainrings goes on the RH side.

3. Install the washer.

4. Install the bolt or the nut · and tighten it fully, then install the dust cap.

5. Firmly retighten the connection after about 40 km (25 miles).

Note on Cottered Cranks:
See the illustration to the left for this type of attachment, which is still used on low-end bikes. If the crank comes loose, tighten the nut. If the problem persists (or to replace the crank), remove the nut and hammer out the cotter pin, while supporting the crank on something solid. When replacing the cotter pin, take the old one to the shop to make sure you get the right size.

The Bottom Bracket

This is the heart of the drivetrain, installed in the frame's bottom bracket shell. It is made up of the spindle, or axle, to which the cranks are attached, and the ball bearings that allow it to turn smoothly. The conventional BSA, or screwed-in, type has adjustable bearings, whereas the bearings of the cartridge (or sealed) unit are not adjustable, although some models can be adjusted laterally to improve the chain line.

If a cartridge bottom bracket develops play or tightness, the bearing cartridges have to be replaced. Except for special models that are easily removable, you may have to take the bike to a shop to have it overhauled or replaced.

Adjust BSA (Screwed-in) Bottom Bracket

Carry out this work on a BSA, or screwed-in, bottom bracket when the bearings have developed play or when they are too tight.

Tools and equipment:
bottom bracket tools (special wrenches for the lockring and the bearing cups)

Top: Loosening or tightening the lockring.

Center: The lockring fits over the adjustable cup.

Bottom: The bottom bracket spindle exposed with the adjustable cup removed.

Procedure:

1. Remove the LH crank (not necessary if the adjustable cup has flats for use with a wrench).

2. Loosen the lockring on the LH side by about one half turn.

3. Loosen the adjustable bearing cup by turning it a quarter turn counterclockwise if the bearing is too tight, clockwise if it is too loose.

4. Restraining the bearing cup, tighten the lockring, then repeat to fine-tune the adjustment if necessary.

Notes:

☐ Bottom bracket looseness is best detected with the cranks installed, using them for leverage while twisting sideways.

☐ Tightness is best established when the cranks are removed.

☐ If you can get the pin wrench for the adjustable cup ground down so that it fits between the crank and the cup, it will be possible to carry out this adjustment without removing the LH crank.

Overhaul Bottom Bracket

This description applies to BSA bottom brackets. Cartridge-bearing bottom brackets vary from one model to the next and usually require special tools—refer any problems to the bike shop.

Tools and equipment:

crank bolt wrench	cloths
crank extractor	solvent
bottom bracket tools	bearing grease

Dismantling Procedure:

1. Remove the LH and RH cranks.

2. Loosen and remove the lockring on the LH side.

3. Loosen and remove the adjustable bearing cup with the pin wrench (or, on older models, with a matching thin open-ended wrench), catching the bearing balls, which are usually held in a retainer.

4. Pull the spindle out, also catching the bearing balls on the other side.

Overhauling Procedure:

1. Clean and inspect all parts, watching for corrosion, wear and damage—grooved or pitted bearing surfaces.

2. If there is serious damage or wear, also check the condition of the fixed (RH) bearing cup, which otherwise

remains on the bike. Except on some imported French and Italian bikes, which have RH thread, the fixed cup invariably has LH threading.

3. Replace any parts that are visibly corroded, damaged or worn, taking the old parts to the shop with you to make sure you get matching replacements.

Installation Procedure:

1. Pack both cleaned bearing cups with bearing grease.

2. If the fixed bearing cup has been removed, reinstall it, turning it counterclockwise.

3. Push the bearing ball retainers into the grease-filled bearing cups, making sure they are installed so that only the balls—not the metal of the retainer—contact the cup.

4. Put the spindle in from the LH side—with the longer end (for the chainring side) first, if it is not symmetric.

5. Install the adjustable cup with its bearing ball retainer in place.

6. Install the lockring.

7. Adjust the bearing as described in the preceding description until it runs smoothly and without play.

Top: Pack the bearing cups with grease and embed the bearing balls in the grease.

Center: The spindle is inserted from the LH side after the fixed cup and its bearing balls have been installed.

Bottom: A cartridge-type bottom bracket is installed as a complete unit, using lockrings or spring clips.

The Chainrings

On a derailleur bike, the chainrings are installed on the RH crank by one of several methods. Once a month, ascertain that the chainrings are still firmly in place by tightening the little bolts that hold them to each other and to the cranks.

Most chainrings are attached with 5 mm Allen bolts, though some models use slotted nuts on one side, for which a slotted screwdriver or hooked tool is used.

Worn chainrings will result in increased resistance and poor shifting. Replace them if they are obviously worn or when teeth are cracked.

If individual teeth are bent, they can sometimes be straightened. When the whole chainring is warped, it can be straightened by carefully using a wedge-shaped block of wood and pushing it between chainstay and chainring or between individual chainrings in the location where they are too close. These jobs can both be done while leaving the chainrings on the bike.

Replace Chainring

This job will be necessary when the chainrings are beyond repair or when you want to change to a different gearing range. First remove the crank, then undo the Allen bolts. The chainrings should not be reversed—remember to replace them facing the right direction. Shimano Superglide and off-round chainrings, such as the now

virtually extinct Shimano Bio-Pace, have a marker that should be lined up with the crank arm for the correct orientation.

The Pedals

Pedals are screwed into the cranks with a normal RH threaded connection on the right, a LH one on the left. They are usually marked R and L, but if you are not certain which pedal goes in which crank arm, do check the threading first.

Pedal maintenance operations are limited to adjustment, overhauling and replacement of a pedal. There are various kinds of toeclips for installation on the pedals, as well as clipless pedals which are becoming increasingly popular.

Replace Pedal

This job may also be necessary when transporting the bike on a plane or a bus. The description is equally valid for regular and clipless pedals.

Tools and equipment:
anti-seize lubricant or grease

pedal wrench or 6 mm Allen wrench

Top and center: The chainrings are usually held onto the RH crank by means of 5 Allen bolts.

Bottom: If they're not too tight, pedals can be removed and installed by means of an Allen wrench on the end of the stub, as shown here. Otherwise you'll have to use a pedal wrench, as shown on page 19.

Removal Procedure:

1. Restrain the crank firmly by straddling the bicycle and placing your foot on either pedal. Place the pedal wrench around the pedal spindle and unscrew the RH pedal counterclockwise, the LH pedal clockwise. Once one pedal is removed, restrain that crank arm as you remove the other pedal.

2. Unscrew the connection between the pedal and the crank. If the pedal has a hexagonal recess in the end of the threaded stub (reached from behind the crank), you may attempt to use the Allen wrench. If the pedal is tight, the Allen wrench may not give sufficient leverage, so you may have to use the special pedal wrench.

Installation Procedure:

1. Clean the threaded hole in the crank and the threaded stub on the pedal, then put some anti-seize or grease on both threaded parts.

2. Carefully align the screw thread and gently screw in the pedal by hand, turning the RH pedal clockwise, the LH pedal counterclockwise.

Note:

If you remove the pedals frequently, I suggest you place a 1–2 mm thin steel washer (again with some grease) between the face of the crank and the pedal stub. This will protect the crank and the thread, making it much easier to loosen and tighten the pedal.

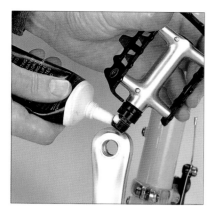

Adjust Pedal Bearings

This description applies only to adjustable-bearing pedals. Cartridge pedals have sealed cartridge bearings that cannot be adjusted but must be replaced at a bike shop when they develop play or resistance.

Tools and equipment:
8–10 mm socket wrench
small screwdriver

dustcap tool, needle-nose
    pliers, or 4–6 mm Allen wrench
grease

Procedure:

1. Remove the dustcap.

2. Loosen the locknut by one turn.

3. Lift the underlying keyed washer with the tip of the screwdriver to loosen it.

4. Using the screwdriver, turn the cone one quarter turn to the right (clockwise) to tighten the bearing, to the left (counterclockwise) to loosen it.

5. Restraining the cone with the screwdriver to make sure it does not turn, tighten the locknut. Add grease if the bearings are dry.

6. Check and readjust if necessary. There should be neither noticeable play nor tightness.

7. Reinstall the dustcap.

Top: Clean the threads of the pedal spindle stub and apply lubricant to any threaded connection that screws into an aluminum part.

Center: The pedal bearing exposed. The outside bearing is the smaller one.

Bottom: A conventional pedal with adjustable bearings dismantled.

Overhaul Pedal

This is required on an adjustable pedal if adjustment does not have the desired effect. Often the problem will be a bent spindle, and then—depending whether such parts are stocked for the model in question—you may have to replace the pedals.

To lubricate or replace the bearings of cartridge-bearing pedals, remove the spindle and the cartridges with the manufacturer's special tool. Pack the cartridge bearings with grease or replace them. If you have difficulty pushing them in, take them to a bike shop to have it done.

Tools and equipment:
dustcap tool, 4–6 mm Allen
    wrench, or needle-nose pliers
8–10 mm socket wrench

small screwdriver
grease
cloth

Dismantling Procedure:

1. Remove the dustcap, preferably using the special tool.

2. Loosen the locknut and remove it.

3. Lift the underlying keyed washer with the tip of the screwdriver to loosen it and then remove it.

4. Using the screwdriver, turn the cone to the left (counter-

Top: Don't ride your bike with the pedal dustcap missing, because dirt and moisture will soon ruin the pedal's bearings.

Center: On some pedals, the cage or quill can be replaced, leaving the mechanism intact.

Bottom: Removing the spindle and bearing from a cartridge-type pedal.

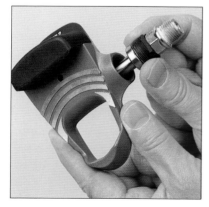

clockwise) to loosen and remove it, catching the bearing balls with the cloth placed underneath the pedal as you do so.

5. Pull the pedal housing off the spindle, also catching the bearing balls on the other side. Count and save all bearing balls. They are quite small and can be easily lost.

Overhauling Procedure:

1. Clean and inspect all bearing surfaces and the pedal axle.

2. Replace anything that is damaged, corroded, grooved or pitted, as well as the pedal spindle if it is bent— or the whole pedal if no spares are available.

3. To make sure you get the right parts when replacing pedal parts or bearing balls, take the old ones to the bike shop for comparison.

Reassembly Procedure:

1. Fill both bearing cups with grease and push the bearing balls into this bed of grease, making sure there is just a little room between —one less than the maximum that might seem to go in at a pinch.

2. Put the pedal housing on the spindle with the larger side (the end without the dustcap screw threading) first—toward the crank.

3. After you've made sure you have not lost any bearing balls, install the adjustable cone.

4. Install the keyed washer with the key fitting in the groove in the pedal spindle.

5. Install the locknut, while restraining the cone so it does not turn with it.

6. Adjust the bearing as described above.

7. Install the dustcap.

Clipless Pedals

In recent years, clipless pedals have become increasingly popular and are now available both for road bikes and for mountain bikes. They invariably run on cartridge bearings. The most important maintenance operation is exterior cleaning with water and a fine brush.

The clipless pedal can be replaced following the same instructions that apply to ordinary pedals. To lubricate or replace the bearings, first remove the bearing cartridge with the manufacturer's special tool. Pack the cartridge bearings with grease if they are accessible, or replace them in their entirety if they are not.

Above: To take the chain apart, push one of the link pins out with the chain tool—but not quite all the way.

The Chain

All derailleur bikes are equipped with a narrow 3/32 in. x 1/2 in. chain. Many single-speed and hub-geared bikes use the wider 1/8 in. x 1/2 in. chain with a connector clip link, often referred to as a master link. The life expectancy of a chain under off-road conditions is limited to about 6 months—even less if you ride a lot in mud, sand and dirt.

Clean and lubricate the chain as described in the section *Preventive Maintenance* in Chapter 3, depending on the kind of weather and terrain you ride in. From time to time, remove the chain to rinse it out in a solvent with 5–10% lubricating oil mixed in, and then lubricate it thoroughly. In the following section, we shall cover removal and installation of the chain.

Sometimes, when shifting problems occur after the bike has been in a spill, the reason will be a twisted chain. This may happen when the derailleur was twisted, trapping the chain in place. Check for this and replace the chain if it is twisted.

When selecting a new chain, make sure you get one that is particularly narrow if your bike has 7 or 8 cogs in the back. I find that drivetrains with Shimano Hyperglide freewheel and Superglide chainrings work just as well with other narrow chains as with the special Hyperglide chain.

Replace Chain

This has to be done whenever you replace the chain or remove it for a thorough cleaning job. Some derailleur maintenance operations are best done with the chain removed from the bike. The Shimano Hyperglide chain, which is specially designed to match the same company's special tooth shape on the chainrings and cogs, requires special attention. That will be covered in a note at the end of the description.

Below: Cleaning and lubricating the chain can be done with this special chain-cleaning tool. But you can also remove the chain and clean it in a can of kerosene, then lubricate it with special chain lubricant.

Tools and equipment: chain rivet extractor
                                  cloths

Fig. 6.2
Chain construction details

Above: To disengage the chain links once the pin has been pushed out far enough, gently twist the chain open.

Below: On Shimano Hyperglide chains, the end of the special link used to make the connection must be removed with pliers, so that it does not get jammed up in the derailleurs.

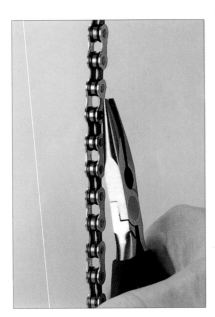

Removal Procedure:

1. Turn the cranks with the rear wheel lifted off the ground and shift gears to put the chain on the smallest chainring in the front and one of the smallest cogs at the back.

2. Place the chain rivet extractor on one of the pins between two links with the punch firmly up against the chain link pin. Retract the handle of the chain rivet extractor and place the chain in the slot farthest from the handle.

3. Turn in the handle by 6 turns, pushing the pin toward the opposite side.

4. Turn the handle back until the tool can be removed.

5. Try to separate the chain at this point by twisting it sideways. If this does not work, reinstall the tool and give it another turn until the chain comes apart. Make sure the pin does not come out altogether—if it does, replace the last inner and outer link at the end.

Installation procedure:

1. Set the derailleurs for the smallest chainring in the front and the second smallest or smallest cog in the back.

2. Wrap the chain around the chainring, cog and derailleur, also passing through the front derailleur cage.

3. There should be just a little spring tension in the rear derailleur, which will tend to pull the chain tighter.

4. If the chain is too long, remove the links in sets of two—the outside link and the link within. Save these for spares.

5. Using the chain rivet extractor from the side where the pin protrudes, push the pin back in until it projects equally on both sides.

6. Twist the chain sideways a few times until it has come loose enough at this point to bend as freely as at the other links. If this can't be

done, put the tool on the chain in the other slot closest to the handle and turn the handle against the pin just a little until the links are freed.

General Note:
If you should accidentally push the pin out all the way when disassembling, replace a section of two links, after removing two more links—taking care not to lose the pin this time. Use a section of the same make and type of chain.

Hyperglide Note:
The Shimano Hyperglide chain has one slightly oversize chain link pin that can be recognized because the link is black, and the chain should not be separated there. Instead split it anywhere else, and remove the pin all the way, then replace it with a special, longer, black pin that is available with the chain or as a replacement. Remove the end of this pin with pliers and file off the pointed end of

Above: The ideal chain line would be a straight line exactly parallel to the plane of the bike's frame.

Below: Modern cassette-type freewheel. This unit actually contains the rear wheel's RH bearing.

this special link before trying out the gears.

Spring Clip Link Note:
To replace the wider chain used on many simple bikes without derailleur gearing, make sure the clip on the special link that is used to connect the two ends is installed in the correct direction (the closed end should travel forward). The spring clip can be lifted with a screwdriver and then prized off (and later put back on) with needle-nose pliers. Adjust the chain length and tension so that the chain can be moved up or down by a total of 2 cm (¾ in). If necessary, fine-tune by installing the wheel farther to the back or the front in the drop-outs.

Chain Line

Ideally, the chain should run parallel to a line through the center of the bike's frame and wheels. On derailleur bikes this means that the point in the middle of the chainrings should be in line with the middle of the set of cogs on the rear hub. To achieve that, it may be possible to adjust the bottom bracket cups sideways. On non-derailleur bikes, the chainring should be in line with the cog. This can often be achieved by reversing the cog, or it may call for a differently shaped cog. Sometimes a parallel line can only be realized by straightening the frame (if the problem is due to misalignment).

The Freewheel

Until recently, most manufacturers used a freewheel block with up to 7 cogs (also called sprockets), screwed on the screw thread of the rear hub. However, in recent years, cassette-hubs, such as the Shimano Freehub, have come to dominate the market. On these models, the freewheel mechanism is integrated in a cassette attached to the rear hub with a large internal hollow Allen bolt, while up to 8 cogs are placed on the splined surface of this cassette and held together by means of a threaded ring or a threaded smallest cog.

As far as the guts of a freewheel mechanism are concerned, I shall not go into any detail here. If the freewheel doesn't work, get a new one (or a new freewheel cassette, in the case of the cassette hub). What is more important is knowing how to lubricate the mechanism, how to exchange cogs and how to remove a complete freewheel block or cassette. Those are the subjects that will be covered here.

Freewheel Lubrication

Do this job if the freewheel block is running roughly, yet is not so old that it seems reasonable to replace it—I suggest once a year. For cassette-type freewheels, first remove the wheel axle and wheel bearings, starting from the RH side, then use a special tool called Freehub-Buddy that is screwed into the end of the cassette body.

Tools and equipment:
SAE 40 or thicker oil

old can or similar receptacle
brush and cloth

Above: A freewheel tool is inserted in the splined ring in the center of the freewheel block to remove it in the case of a screwed-on freewheel.

Below: In the case of many cassette-type hubs, it is also used together with a chain whip to remove the smallest cog or the lockring on top.

Procedure:

1. Before you lubricate the mechanism, clean the cogs, the spaces between them, and the visible end of the freewheel, preferably with the wheel removed from the bike. This can be done using an old cloth or stiff brush.

2. On freewheel blocks with an oil hole, add oil until it oozes out at the other end.

3. On a freewheel without an oil hole, put the wheel on its side with the freewheel facing up, and a receptacle under the hub to catch excess oil. Turn the hub relative to the wheel, and introduce oil into the gap that is visible between stationary and turning parts of the freewheel mechanism—until it comes out clean on the other side.

4. Let it drip until no more oil comes out, then clean off excess oil.

Replace Screwed-on Freewheel

Once the wheel is removed from the bicycle, you can usually tell a freewheel block from a freewheel cassette, because on the former models there will be internal splines or notches into which a freewheel tool fits.

Tools and equipment:

freewheel tool   10-in. crescent wrench
spanner or vise   grease

Removal Procedure:

1. Remove the rear wheel from the bike.

2. Remove the quick-release or the axle nut and its washer on the RH side.

3. Place the freewheel tool on the freewheel with the ribs or prongs on the tool exactly matching the splines or notches in the freewheel body.

4. Install the quick-release or the RH axle nut, leaving a 2 mm ($\frac{3}{32}$ in.) space in order to hold the tool in place.

5. If you have a vice, clamp the tool in with the side matching the freewheel facing up; if not, place the wrench on the flat faces of the tool and clamp the wheel securely, with the tire pushed against the floor and one wall of the room. Be careful when using SunTour removers to avoid breaking off their fragile prongs.

6. Turn the wheel counter-clockwise to loosen the screw thread between hub and freewheel. Forcefully turn either the wheel relative to the vise, or the wrench relative to the wheel—about one turn, until the space between the tool and the nut is taken up.

7. Loosen the nut another 2 turns and repeat this process until the freewheel

Above and below: Cassette disassembly. Once the top cog, or in this case the lockring, has been removed, the other cogs just lift off. (In case of the Shimano XTR mountain bike cassette, the four bigger cogs may be combined in one set and screwed onto a central spider to save weight.)

can be removed by hand, (after you have removed the axle nut or the quick-release).

Installation Procedure:

1. Clean the threaded surfaces of the freewheel block (inside) and the hub (outside), and coat these surfaces with grease to prevent corrosion and to ease subsequent removal.

2. Put the wheel down horizontally with the threaded end facing up.

3. Carefully screw the freewheel block on by hand, making sure that it is correctly threaded on, until it cannot be tightened further that way.

4. Install the wheel, and allow the driving force to "automatically" tighten it as you ride.

Replace Cassette Freewheel

If no internal notches or splines to take a tool are visible, you probably have a cassette-type freewheel. It is held inside the rear hub with an internal Allen bolt.

Tools and equipment: 9 or 10 mm Allen wrench

Removal Procedure:

1. Disassemble the hub bearing on the LH side, and remove the axle.

2. Hold the wheel firmly and unscrew the freewheel cassette (with its cogs) with the big Allen wrench (10 mm for Shimano, 9 mm for Sun-Tour and Campagnolo).

Installation Procedure:

1. Carefully clean and very lightly lubricate the thread of the freewheel cassette and the hole in the hub.

2. Accurately place the freewheel cassette (with its cogs) in the hub.

3. Tighten the freewheel cassette with the big Allen wrench.

Note:
If the wheel locks up, it is probably because the internal Allen bolt is not tightened down fully. To correct this problem, remove the RH locknut and cone, then pull the axle from the LH side and tighten the freewheel cassette with the 9 or 10 mm Allen wrench. Then reassemble.

Above: The cassette freewheel body can be separated from the rear hub, after the LH bearing and the wheel axle have been removed, using a 9 or 10 mm Allen wrench, depending on the make.

Below: On conventional freewheel blocks, two chain whips are used to remove the cogs.

Replace Cog on Cassette Freewheel

On these units, the cogs are held in splines on the freewheel cassette, held together with a lockring (Shimano) or a screwed-on smallest cog (SunTour and Campagnolo).

On Shimano Hyperglide cogs, which owe their easy shifting to subtle alignment of specially shaped teeth, one of the splines is wider, so make sure you line them up properly.

Tools and equipment:
2 chain whips (cog wrenches)

freewheel tool (Shimano)
10-in. adjustable wrench

Dismantling Procedure:

1. Remove the wheel from the bike.

2. Place the wheel horizontally in front of you with the freewheel cassette facing up.

3. On Shimano Hyperglide models, use the chain whip to restrain the largest cog while using the freewheel tool to unscrew the locking cog. Other freewheel cassettes can be removed with two chain whips by simply turning the last (smallest) cog against the biggest one.

4. Remove the cogs and the spacers, noting the sequence of the various cogs and spacers.

Installation procedure:

1. Install the cogs and the spacers in the same sequence.

2. Screw on the last cog or the notched ring, while countering with a chain whip wrapped around one of the other cogs on road models.

3. Use the freewheel tool to install the lockring on Shimano Hyperglide models.

Note on Shimano XTR:
On these lightweight cassette freewheel hubs, the larger cogs are installed on a stepped "spider" and are held with 3 long bolts. To replace them, unscrew the lockring using the freewheel tool, and remove the smaller cogs first.

Replace Cog on Screwed-on Freewheel

On these conventional units, most or all of the cogs are screwed onto the freewheel. The procedure is similar to that outlined for the cassette freewheel, except that you will always need two chain whips, one wrapped around the smallest cog, one around one of the other cogs. When you have finished reassembly, put the chain on the smallest cog and stand on the pedals to tighten it. Then readjust the derailleur, if necessary.

CHAPTER 7

The Wheels

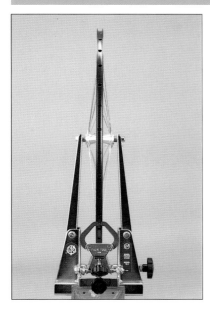

Above: Perfectly round and perfectly aligned: the ideal in bicycle wheels.

Below: Close-up look at a mountain bike wheel with knobby tire and quick-release hub.

Bottom right: A collection of road and mountain bike wheels.

THE bicycle wheel consists of hub, rim, tire, tube, and spokes. One end of the spokes is hooked onto the hub flange, and the other end is connected with the rim by means of a screwed-on nipple. The ends of the spokes and the nipples are covered with a strip of rim tape to protect the tube. This tape is concealed by the tire and the tube.

Wheel problems are the primary cause of bicycle breakdowns, especially if you ride off-road frequently. In this chapter we shall cover all the major maintenance and repair operations required.

First you will be shown how to replace the wheel most effectively, as is often necessary to transport the bike or to carry out other maintenance jobs.

Replace Wheel with Quick-Release

Quick-release hubs are now used extensively on road bikes and mountain bikes alike.

Tools and equipment: cloth (for rear wheel)

Removal Procedure:

1. If you are working on the rear wheel, first put the chain on the smallest cog and the smallest chainring by means of the derailleur, while turning the cranks with the wheel raised off the ground.

2. If your tire is flat, it will easily pass between the brake pads.

Above: Operation of the quick-release. The skewer can only lock the wheel in firmly if you notice a definite resistance just before the lever reaches the closed position, followed by a snapping action.

Below: Open up the brake to allow the wheel to slip between the brake pads—unless you have a punctured tire.

3. To allow an inflated tire to pass between the brake pads, release the brake. On road bikes that is done by flipping the brake quick-release. On mountain bikes it is done by squeezing the brake arms against the rim and unhooking the straddle cable QR nipple (on a canti-lever brake or a U-brake) or by twisting the cam plate out (on the roller-cam brake). In the case of an under-the-chainstay U-brake, just push the wheel forward in the drop-outs until it hits the inside of the brake, spreading the brake arms apart.

4. Twist the hub's quick-release lever to the "open" position.

5. On the rear wheel, pull back the derailleur and the chain, using a cloth to keep your hands clean. Pull out the wheel, guiding it past the brake pads.

Installation Procedure:

1. If you are working on the rear wheel, first put the shifters in the position to engage the gear with the chain on the smallest cog and the smallest chainring. Turn the cranks forward if you have to engage another chainring in the front.

2. To allow the tire to pass be-tween the brake pads, make sure the brake is released—if not, squeeze the brake arms together and unhook one of the QR nipples (on a can-tilever brake or a U-brake) or twist the cam plate out (on a roller-cam brake).

3. Twist the lever on the hub's quick-release to the "open" position.

4. On the rear wheel, pull back the derailleur and the chain.

5. Slide the wheel back into position, guiding it past the brake pads.

6. Straighten the wheel exact-ly between fork blades or be-tween chain stays and seat stays.

7. Holding the wheel in the correct position, flip the quick-release lever to the "closed" position and make sure the wheel is locked firmly in place.

8. Verify you have installed the wheel perfectly centered.

9. Tension the brake or reinstall the QR nipple, then readjust the brake.

Replace Wheel with Axle Nuts

Still used on many roadsters and other low-end bikes, the attach-ment by means of axle nuts is in no way inferior. Here's how to go about removing and installing such a wheel.

Tools and equipment: 13 or 15 mm wrench
cloth

Above: Hold back the chain with the derailleur to remove the rear wheel.

Below: If the drop-outs have adjusting screws, use them to fix the rear wheel hub position so the wheel stays aligned perfectly straight.

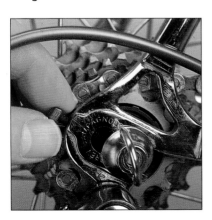

Removal Procedure

1. If you are working on the rear wheel, first put the chain on the smallest cog and the smallest chainring by means of the derailleur, while turning the cranks with the rear wheel raised off the ground.

2. To allow the tire to pass between the brake pads, release the brake by squeezing the brake arms against the rim and unhook the straddle cable's QR nipple (on a cantilever brake or a U-brake) or twist the cam plate out (on the roller-cam brake). On a mountain bike with a U-brake mounted under the chainstays, push the wheel forward against the inside of the brake to spread the brake arms apart.

3. Loosen both axle nuts by 2 or 3 turns.

4. On the rear wheel, pull back the derailleur and the chain.

5. Pull out the wheel, guiding it past the brake pads.

Installation Procedure:

1. If you are working on the rear wheel, first put the shifters in the position to engage the gear with the chain on the smallest cog and the smallest chainring. Turn the cranks forward if you have to engage another chainring in the front.

2. To allow the tire to pass between the brake shoes, make sure the the brake is released—if not, open the quick-release (on road bike brakes) or squeeze the brake arms together and unhook the straddle cable's QR nipples (on a cantilever brake or a U-brake) or twist the cam plate out (on the roller-cam brake).

3. Install the washers (if the axle nuts do not have

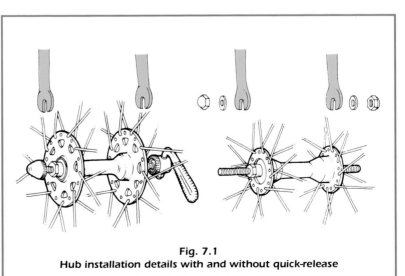

Fig. 7.1
Hub installation details with and without quick-release

Above: *Use a cone wrench in conjunction with a second wrench on the opposite* locknut *to tighten the bearing, on the opposite* cone *to loosen it.*

Below: *To tighten or loosen the locknut, restrain the underlying cone with a second wrench.*

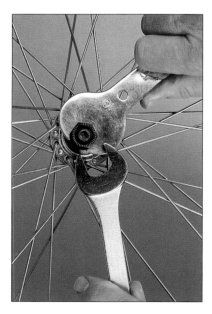

integral washers) between the drop-outs and the nuts.

4. On the rear wheel, pull back the derailleur and the chain.

5. Slide the wheel back into position, guiding it past the brake pads, and center the rim exactly between fork blades or between chain stays and seat stays.

6. Holding the wheel in place at the brake, first tighten the axle nuts one after the other by hand, then tighten them gradually with the wrench.

7. Verify you have installed the wheel in the right position and correct if necessary.

8. Tension the brake or reinstall the straddle cable's QR nipple, then readjust the brake to make sure the brake pads touch the sides of the rim fully and equally when the brake lever is applied.

The Hub

Hubs should be checked occasionally to make sure they still turn freely and are not too loose. Maintenance will consist of adjustment, lubrication and overhauling when necessary. Cartridge hubs require specialized tools; some are adjustable.

You can maximize the life of a hub by means of regular checks, adjustment, lubrication and overhauling. To replace a hub, the entire wheel has to be rebuilt, which runs the bill up considerably. Besides, many models are only available as pairs, effectively doubling the cost.

Hub Bearing Check

This procedure applies to any kind of hub, whether it is the conventional adjustable-bearing type or a cartridge-bearing model.

Tools and Equipment: Usually none required.

Procedure:

1. To check whether the hub runs freely, merely lift the wheel off the ground and let it spin slowly. It should rotate several times and then oscillate gradually into the motionless state with the (slightly heavier) valve at the bottom. If it does not turn freely, adjust the bearings to loosen them (and probably they should be lubricated as well).

2. To check whether there is play in the bearings, grab the rim close to the brake with one hand, while holding at the fork or the stays with the other, and try to push the rim sideways in both directions. If it moves loosely, the hub bearing should be tightened.

Above: Close-up view of a front wheel hub with plastic seals to keep out as much dirt and water as possible.

Below: Once the cone is removed, you should see the bearing balls, one hopes embedded in grease, in the bearing cup.

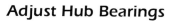

Adjust Hub Bearings

Carry out this work when the preceding test indicates a need for readjustment. In the case of a rear hub, first remove the freewheel (see Chapter 6) unless it is a cassette hub. The first step after removing the freewheel should be to tighten the locknut on the drive side (RH side) firmly up against the underlying cone.

Tools and equipment:
13–16 mm cone wrench　　　13–15 mm open ended or ring wrenches

Procedure:

1. Remove the wheel or, if it is the type with axle nuts, merely loosen the axle nut on one side if you want to leave the wheel installed on the bike.

2. Loosen the locknut on one side by one turn, countering by holding the cone on the same side of the wheel with the cone wrench.

3. Tighten or loosen the cone by about a quarter turn at a time until the bearing is just a little loose. To loosen, counter at the cone on the other side with an open-ended wrench. To tighten, counter at the *locknut* on the other side.

4. Hold the cone with the cone wrench and tighten the locknut hard up against it, which will slightly decrease the play.

5. Check and readjust if necessary.

6. Reinstall the wheel on the bike—or just tighten the axle nut if you loosened it on one side only.

Lubricate Hub Bearing

Once a season, or whenever adjusting will not solve the hub's problems, lubricate the hub in a big way as described below under *Overhaul Hub.* In between, many high-quality hubs can be quickly lubricated through an oil hole provided in the hub shell, which is covered by a spring clip. Use a special lubricant or SAE 60 oil, filled in a pressure oil can with a very narrow spout. Other bearings can be packed with grease after the plastic seals are lifted with a narrow screwdriver. Cartridge hubs require a little light oil under the seals to run smoothly.

Overhaul Hub

Do this work when the bearings of the hub are no longer running smoothly and cannot be returned to proper working order by means of adjustment and lubrication.

Tools and equipment:
13–16 mm cone wrenches　　　cloths
13–15 mm ring wrenches　　　bearing grease

Above: On a cassette-type rear hub, the RH wheel bearing actually lies in the freewheel cassette—start disassembly from the opposite side.

Below: Close-up view of the spoked-in rim of a wheel, showing the nipples recessed in the rim. On this model, the first spoke hole counted clockwise from the valve hole is off-set to the left.

Dismantling Procedure:

1. Remove the wheel from the bike.

2. Remove the quick-release or the axle nuts and washers.

3. Remove the locknut on one side, countering by holding the cone on the *same* side.

4. Lift off the lock washer.

5. Remove the cone, countering by holding the cone on the *other* side. Catch the bearing balls as you remove the cone.

6. Pull the axle (with the other cone, washer and locknut still installed at the other end) out of the hub shell, again catching the bearing balls and removing the plastic seal (if installed) from the hub shell.

Overhauling Procedure:

1. Clean and inspect all bearing parts.

2. Replace the bearing balls with new ones of the same size, and replace any other parts that may be damaged (pitted, grooved or corroded surfaces).

Reassembly Procedure:

1. First fill the clean bearing cups in the hub with bearing grease, then reinstall the dust seals.

2. Push the bearing balls into the grease, filling the circumference but leaving enough space to move freely. A rule of thumb is to use one ball less than might fill the cup.

3. Insert the axle with one cone, washer and locknut still installed. If you are working on a rear wheel, make sure it goes the same way round as it did originally.

4. Screw the other cone onto the free axle end, until the bearings seem just a little loose.

5. Install the lock washer with its key in the axle groove.

6. Screw the locknut on and tighten it against the cone.

7. Check and, if necessary, adjust the bearing as described above until it runs well.

8. Reinstall the wheel on the bike.

Note:
If you replace the cones, make sure the axle protrudes equally far on both sides—reposition both cones and locknuts to achieve this if necessary.

Rim and Spokes

These two parts have to be treated together, since the spoke tension determines largely whether the rim is straight and true or not. The spokes connect the rim to the hub in one of the patterns referred to as radial, 2-cross, 3-cross and 4-cross spoking. Almost any pattern

Above: Spokes of different gauges, or thicknesses, each require a particular size spoke wrench. It's best to use color-coded ones in preference to a single wrench with a range of different size slots.

Below: For a fast wheel-building or truing job, you need a truing stand with reference gauges to show where the rim is off-set.

is suitable for the front wheel, which does not transmit any torque; the rear wheel should have a 3- or 4-cross pattern, at least on the RH, or chain side. If you are a heavy rider or ride on rough roads, don't use wheels with fewer than 36 spokes—at least in the rear.

You can minimize wheel problems, most typically broken spokes and bent rims, by keeping the spokes tensioned adequately. Check the feel and the sound of plucking a well-tensioned new wheel at a bike shop and compare yours. If necessary, increase the tension of all or some spokes, following the procedure outlined in the following section on wheel truing.

Wheel Truing Check

When a wheel is damaged, the rim is often permanently deformed sideways, resulting in wheel wobble. This can be detected as lateral oscillations when riding. Verify this by turning the wheel slowly while it is lifted off the ground, observing the distance between the rim and a fixed point on the frame's rear triangle or on the fork. On a properly trued wheel, this distance is the same on both sides of the wheel and does not vary as the wheel is turned.

Emergency Repair of Buckled Wheel

Sometimes the damage is so serious that you don't need to check: it will be obvious that the wheel is buckled—and there is little you can do to solve the problem permanently or even temporarily with adequate certainty to be safe. However, such a seriously bent wheel can often be straightened enough to ride home—carefully.

Support the rim at the low point and push down forcefully on the high points. Check frequently and continue until the whole thing at least looks like a wheel. Then follow the procedure for *Wheel Truing* to fine-tune the wheel far enough to be able to ride it home. Have it corrected or replaced as soon as possible.

Wheel Truing and Stress Relieving

This is the work done to get a bent wheel back into shape. It is most easily done at home, but can be carried out after a fashion by the roadside—at least well enough to get you home. In the home workshop, it is preferable to do this job using a truing stand, but it can be done with the wheel in the frame, preferably with the bike upside-down (but with the handlebars supported so nothing gets damaged). It is best to remove the tire and the tube first, but this is not essential.

Tools and equipment: spoke wrench

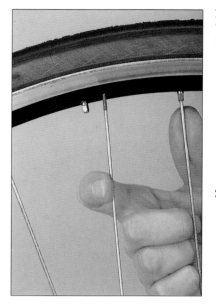

Above: Replacing a single spoke. Sometimes, if the nipple is still in good shape, you can leave the tire on the wheel, although you should let the air escape first if your wheel has a rim on which the nipples protrude from the rim's tire well.

Below: A professional wheel centering gauge allows you to quickly check whether the wheel is properly centered relative to the hub.

Procedure:

1. Slowly spin the wheel while watching a fixed reference point on both sides, such as the gauge on the truing stand—or the bicycle's brake pads if you are working without a truing stand. Mark the locations that have to be moved farther to the left and the right.

2. Using the spoke wrench, loosen the nipples of the spokes on the high side in the area of a high spot, and tighten those on the opposite side, in the same area. Turn the ones in the middle of the high spot a half turn, and those farther from the center only a quarter turn at a time. This is easy, since the nipples have a square flattened area for the tool.

3. Your wheel must be properly centered once you have trued it. This is checked by using a dishing tool or the brake pads for a reference point. If the wheel is off center, tighten all the spokes on one side in quarter-turn steps, and loosen the opposing spokes in quarter-turn steps to center the rim on the axle. Always begin and end at the valve hole so you don't miss any spokes.

4. Once you have achieved an improved spoke line, you must stress-relieve the spokes. This is done by grasping parallel spoke pairs on both sides of the wheel and squeezing them together working around the wheel, starting and finishing at the valve hole.

5. Continue this process for each off-set area, checking and correcting frequently, until the wheel is quite well trued.

6. On the rear wheel of a derailleur bike, the spokes on the RH side will be at a steeper angle, and consequently under a higher tension, than those on the LH side. This is because the hub flanges are laterally asymmetrical due to the freewheel on the RH side.

Note:

The first time you true a wheel, it will take forever and still may not lead to a really satisfactory result. Persist, and the next time will be easier. Just the same, the first few times you do this, have a bike mechanic check your work.

Replace Spokes

Sometimes a spoke breaks—usually at the head, which is hooked in at the hub flange. Make sure you have replacement spokes of the same thickness and the same length.

Tools and equipment:
spoke wrenches

tools to remove freewheel or cogs of cassette hub.

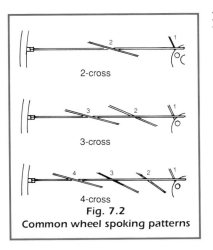

Fig. 7.2
Common wheel spoking patterns

Above: Spoking a wheel in the truing stand. As an alternative, you can make do with holding the wheel in the fork or the rear drop-outs while you are working on it, using the brake pads as reference points.

Procedure:

1. Remove the screwed-on freewheel or the freewheel cassette (refer to Chapter 6), tire, tube and rim tape. Unscrew nipple of broken spoke with spoke wrench.

2. Hook the spoke through the hole in the hub—with the head on the inside of the flange if this will be an out-side spoke, on the outside if it will be an inside spoke.

3. Regardless which spoking pattern, count 4 spokes along the circumference of the rim to find a spoke that is routed the same way as your spoke will have to be. Refer to this one to find out just how to run it and how it should cross the other spokes.

4. Route your spoke the same way as the example.

5. Screw the nipple onto the threaded end of the spoke, slowly increasing tension until it is about as tight as all other spokes on the same side of the same wheel.

6. Follow the procedure given under *Wheel Truing* until the wheel is perfectly true.

7. Replace tire, tube and rim tape. Inflate the tire.

Note:
If only one spoke is broken, and you happen to be without a spare spoke, true the wheel around the broken spoke by tightening and loosening the op-posing sides. Stress-relieve the wheel, then true it again. If several spokes are broken, you can establish which rim holes and hub flange holes go together by observing that every fourth spoke along the rim, (every second one on the same hub flange), runs similarly.

Emergency Spoke Installation

Make your own emergency spoke by bending an oversized spoke from which you first remove the head to form a hook at one end. It is used to replace a broken spoke on the RH side of the rear wheel, since it can be hooked in without removing the freewheel.

Note:
When you get home, replace this temporary repair by a permanent spoke of the right length, a job you can either do yourself or leave to the bike shop. Warning: an improperly tensioned wheel can go out of true quickly or even collapse, especially if the spokes are too loose. Spokes tensioned too tightly will cause the rim to crack at the nipples.

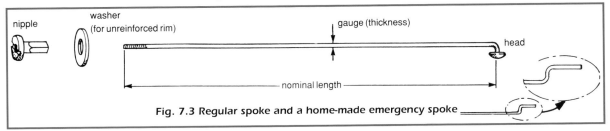

Fig. 7.3 Regular spoke and a home-made emergency spoke

Above: The simple way to replace a rim is by tying the new rim to the old one and moving each spoke to the corresponding location on the new rim. Only recommended if spokes and nipples are still in good condition.

Wheel Spoking

This work is necessary to replace either the rim (in case it is badly bent or damaged) or the hub. Here I will describe only the simple method to replace a rim by a new one using the old hub and spokes. For a more thorough treatment, recommended only for accomplished home mechanics, refer to my *Bicycle Repair Book*.

Make sure the new rim is identical to the old one: Check the size and count the holes in the hub and the rim, and make sure the spoke holes are offset relative to the centerline of the rim in the same pattern (check on either side of the valve hole).

Tools and equipment:

spoke wrench	grease
cloth	adhesive tape

Procedure:

1. Remove the tire, the tube and the rim tape from the old rim on the existing wheel.

2. Place the existing tape on the new rim, with the valve holes lined up.

3. Tape the two rims together between the spoke holes in at least 3 locations.

4. Starting at the first spoke to the right of the valve hole, remove each spoke from the old rim, and immediately install it in the new rim. Screw the nipple on until about 3 mm (1/8 in.) of the spoke screw thread is exposed.

5. After all the spokes have been replaced, work your

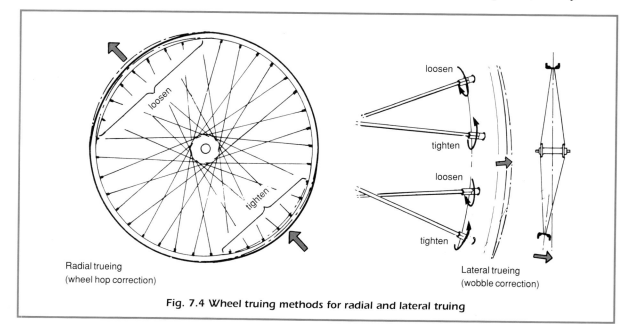

Radial trueing
(wheel hop correction)

Lateral trueing
(wobble correction)

Fig. 7.4 Wheel truing methods for radial and lateral truing

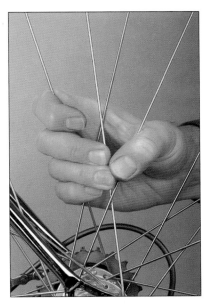

Top: Relieving the spoke stress.

Center: Inserting the tire lever.

Bottom: Taking the valve out.

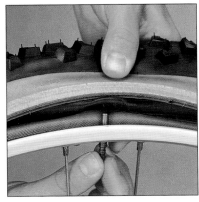

way around the wheel, tightening all the spokes in steps of about one half turn at a time until they are equally tensioned.

6. Follow the description for wheel truing to bring the wheel into lateral and radial true and to tension the spokes until they have about the same tension as those on a new wheel. Pay attention to the need for higher tension on the free-wheel side of a typical rear wheel.

7. Stress-relieve the spokes by grasping them in pairs of parallel spokes, working around the wheel. Center the wheel using a centering device. Or improvise: turn the wheel around and make sure the distance from rim to brake pad stays the same.

8. Check inside the rim and file off any spoke ends that may project from the nipples.

9. Install the new rim tape, the tire and the tube. Inflate the tire and retrue the wheel, if necessary.

10. Check and retension the wheel every 40 km (25 miles) for the next 120 km (75 miles).

Tire and Tube

Tires remain the bicycle's weak spot. I advise carrying a spare tube, a pump and a repair kit at all times. The tire size is marked on the side wall and must match the rim. On virtually all mountain bikes, rims with a diameter of 559 mm are used, requiring tires of a corresponding size. The international standard size designation is ISO or ETRTO, which references this rim diameter and the width of its cross-section. US manufacturers designate tires by their nominal outside diameter and width.

The width of the tire is important in matching machine and terrain: though relatively narrow tires are acceptable for riding on well-surfaced roads, the widest MTB-tires with a nominal width of 2.125 in. (54 mm) are needed for really rough terrain, as well as for loose sand, snow or other soft surfaces. Not every tire width can necessarily be installed on every frame or every rim. When installed, there should be at least 6 mm (¼ in.) clearance between inflated tire and frame stays or fork blades on both sides on a mountain bike, at least 4 mm on a road bike. Ideally, the inner tube should match the tire, though you will find that most tubes fit most tires of the same nominal diameter.

Puncture Repair

Mending a punctured or "flat" tire is required more frequently than any other repair, and every cyclist should be able to handle this simple job. Whether you actually repair the old tube or install a new one is up to you, but you can't carry unlimited spares, so you will be confronted with the need to repair the leak yourself sooner or later. Though the description involves many steps, the work is not difficult

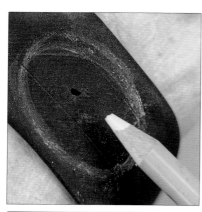

Top: Mark the location of the hole.

Center: Roughen and clean the area.

Bottom: Apply rubber solution.

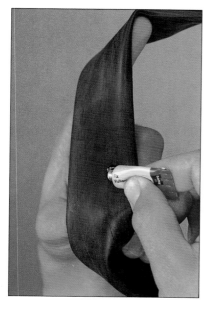

and can, with some practice, be handled in about ten minutes, even out on the trail.

The whole thing is expedited considerably if the tire fits on the rim rather loosely. That is typically taken care of by selecting rims with a deep bed and trying out the tire for fit. In fact, on mountain bikes, it is often possible to remove the tire by hand without the need for tire levers.

Tools and equipment:

tire repair kit

tire levers

spare tube

13–15 mm wrench

small screwdriver

Procedure:

1. Check the valve. Try to inflate and check whether air is escaping there. Sometimes a Schrader valve will leak and can be fixed by screwing in the interior, using a narrow object, like a small screwdriver. Presta valves will leak if the top nut isn't screwed on.

2. If it is a rear wheel, select a gear that combines a small cog with a small chainring.

3. Remove the wheel from the bike, holding back chain and rear derailleur. You may have to release the brake for the tire to clear the brake pads.

4. Check the circumference of the tire for visible signs of damage, and mark their location with a ballpoint pen or by tying something around the nearest spoke.

5. If the tire still contains air, push the valve pin in (Schrader), or first unscrew the nut, then push the valve pin in (Presta). This will allow all trapped air to escape.

6. To loosen the tire, push one side of the tire toward the (deeper) tire well in the center of the rim around the entire circumference of the wheel to loosen that side enough to ease removal.

7. If it does not come off by hand, place the longer end of a tire lever under the side of the tire and hook the short end under a spoke.

8. Two or three spokes farther round the rim, insert the second tire lever.

9. Insert the third tire lever 2 or 3 spokes in the opposite direction (if you have only two levers, remove one of the two and use it in the new location).

10. Remove the tire levers. Starting at the location of the tire levers, pull the rest of the same side of the tire off by hand.

11. Remove the tube from under the tire, pushing the valve out of the valve hole.

12. Check the tube, starting at any location you may have marked as an obvious or probable cause of the puncture.

13. If the leak is not easily detected, inflate the tire and check carefully for

Above: After removing the foil backing from the patch's adhesive side, apply the patch to the treated area of the tube. Center it over the hole.

Below: The patch must adhere fully. Start all over again if it comes off in even one small area.

escaping air, passing the tube by your eye, which is your most sensitive detection device. To date, I have not encountered a leak that could not be found this way, but it takes some practice.

14. If you are not able to detect escaping air, submerge the inflated tire in water or, if not enough of that is available, rub a little water from your water bottle over the inflated tire, systematically working around and re-inflating the tire as required to maintain adequate pressure.

15. Mark the location of the leak.

16. Take an appropriate patch from the patch kit. Generally, the smallest size will do, unless you are dealing with several holes close together or with a long tear.

17. If you had to dip it in water, dry the tube around the leak. Roughen the area around the leak with abrasive paper from the patch kit and wipe clean.

18. Take a sizeable drop of rubber solution from the tube in the patch kit and quickly spread it smoothly and evenly over an area around the leak that is a little larger than the patch.

19. Allow the rubber solution to dry one minute for a normal butyl tube, twice that long if you have a latex tube.

20. Remove the plastic or aluminum foil from the adhesive side of the patch without touching the ad-

hesive, and quickly yet accurately place the patch on the area prepared, centered at the leak.

21. Push the patch down, then knead and flex patch and tube together to make sure the patch adheres fully. If not, remove it and restart at step 16.

22. Inflate the tube partway to establish whether air escapes. If it does, there may be another hole or the first one was not patched properly. Repeat the repair if necessary.

23. Inflate the tube to verify whether it holds air. Meanwhile, check the inside of the tire to find and remove any embedded objects that may have caused the puncture—or may cause subsequent ones. Thorns are particularly tricky, since they wear off and become almost invisible on the outside and undetectable inside; yet they may protrude far enough inside to pierce the tube when the tire is compressed.

24. Check inside the rim to make sure none of the spokes protrude and that they are covered by rim tape. Once at home, file off any spokes that do protrude, and replace or patch defective rim tape. You can use duct tape to mend a broken rim tape.

25. When you are sure the problem is solved, let most of the air escape from the tube until it is limp.

Above: Carefully put the tube back on the rim under the tire, and pull the tire sidewall over the rim.

Below: Sometimes a tire casing can be patched, but this one is probably too far gone for a permanent repair.

26. Starting at the valve, put the tube back under the tire, over the rim.

27. Pull the side of the tire back over the rim, starting opposite the valve and working in both directions toward the valve.

28. If the tube has a Presta valve, reinstall the knurled locknut. Whatever the valve, make sure it is straight.

29. Inflate the tire partway and check once more to make sure the tube is not pinched. Knead the tire sidewalls from both sides, and make sure the tire is centered. The ridge on the sidewall should be equally far from the rim around the circumference on both sides.

30. Inflate the tire to the desired pressure—the narrower the tire, the higher the pressure should be.

Note:
Even if you choose not to patch a tube while you are out on the road, replacing it with your spare tube instead, you should repair the puncture once you get home, so you can use that tube as a spare.

Replace Tube or Tire Casing

If the inner tube cannot be repaired, because the hole is on a seam or too large, or if you want to install another tube for any other reason, proceed as described above for repairing a puncture under steps 2–11, then install the new tube and continue as described under steps 26–30.

To replace the tire itself, initially also proceed as described above in steps 2–10 for repairing a puncture. Then remove the other side of the tire in the same direction as the first side. Put one side of the new tire in place and continue as before.

Patch Tire Casing

Sometimes a damaged tire casing can be repaired at least temporarily. To do so, proceed just as you did for the puncture repair. Repair the inside of the tire, using a 2.5 cm x 5 cm (1 in. x 2 in.) "boot." This can be a piece of duct tape, a piece cut from the side of a discarded lightweight tire, or even a small sheet of plastic if you're desperate.

First put rubber solution on one side of the patch, allowing it to dry, and then reapply rubber solution there *and* in the area of the tire where it has to be repaired. Once it has adhered, generously sprinkle talcum powder over the area of the boot and around it to prevent the tire from sticking to the tube—or place a piece of thin paper between the patch and the tube if you don't want to use talcum powder (some people fear it may be bad for your lungs).

CHAPTER 8

The Steering System

The bicycle's front end contains its steering system. Shown here is a mountain bike, but the same parts are found on any other bike.

THE steering system is crucial for control over the bike. The parts of the steering system are the front fork, the headset bearings, the stem and the handlebars. (The latter two parts are sometimes combined into a single welded unit.) We'll cover each of the components, starting at the most frequently necessary jobs.

Handlebars and Stem

The handlebars are generally clamped in the stem's clamping collar and the stem is held in the fork's steerer tube by means of a wedge-shaped or a cone-shaped device. This is pulled into the bottom of the stem with the expander bolt, accessible from the top of the stem and usually equipped with a 6 mm hexagon recess for an Allen wrench. The collar of the stem is generally also provided with one or more Allen bolts to clamp it around the handlebars, and often a worm screw (i.e., one without a head) to spread the collar apart.

The jobs you may have to do are adjusting the height, straightening the bars, and replacing either part. Most handlebars have a diameter of $\frac{7}{8}$ in. (22.2 mm) at the ends and either 1 in. (25.4 mm), $1\frac{1}{8}$ in. (26.6 mm), 26 mm, or 27 mm at the point where they are clamped into the stem. Make sure stem and handlebars match when replacing either one.

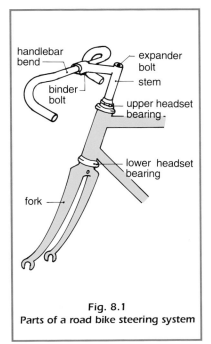

Fig. 8.1
Parts of a road bike steering system

Adjust, Straighten, or Tighten Handlebars

This is required when the bike is set up for a different rider, when the position proves uncomfortable, or when the handlebars are not firmly in place.

Tools and equipment:

6 mm Allen wrench (or 12 mm wrench for older bikes with a hexagon-head expander bolt)

sometimes a mallet or a hammer and a block of wood for protection

Procedure:

1. If the front brake cable is anchored at the stem, first loosen the brake to relax the cable tension.

2. To adjust the handlebar position, loosen the stem by unscrewing the expander bolt 2–3 turns.

Above: Usually, the expander bolt is recessed in the top of the stem and is tightened and loosened with a 6 mm Allen wrench.

Below: The handlebars (or handlebar bend) are held in the stem with one or more binder bolts. The small additional Allen bolt shown here is used to spread the collar open so that the handlebars can be removed or installed.

3. Straddle the front wheel, keeping it straight relative to the bike's frame, and put the handlebars in the required position as regards height and alignment, holding them steady with one hand.

4. If the stem won't turn or move, unscrew the expander bolt 2 more turns; lift the wheel off the ground, supporting the bike from the handlebars, then tap on the expander bolt with the mallet, after which it will usually come loose. If it doesn't, enter some spray lubricant between the stem and the collar or locknut at the top of the headset and try again.

5. Put the handlebars in the desired position. To assure the stem is held securely, check to make sure the stem is not raised so high that the maximum height marker engraved in the stem becomes visible above the headset locknut.

6. Still holding the front wheel and the handlebars firmly, tighten the expander bolt.

7. Verify whether the handlebars are now in the right position and make any corrections that may be necessary.

8. If the brake's adjustment was affected (see step 1 above), tension the cable and adjust the brake.

Tighten Handlebars in Stem

The connection between the handlebars and the stem should also be firm, so the handlebars don't twist out of their proper orientation. To do this, simply tighten the bolts that clamp the stem collar around the bars, using a 5–6 mm Allen wrench. On older models, use a 12 mm wrench to tighten the nut.

Remove and Install Handlebars and Stem Together

This work has to be done in order to work on the headset or to replace the front fork. How the handlebars and the stem are replaced individually will be shown in a subsequent procedure.

Tools and equipment:
5–6 mm Allen wrench (on older bikes, a 12 mm wrench)

cloth
grease
mallet or hammer (sometimes)

Removal Procedure:

1. Loosen and detach brake and gear cables from the levers on the handlebars.

2. Using the 6 mm Allen wrench or the wrench, loosen the expander bolt by

3–4 turns, or until the stem is loose.

3. If the stem won't come loose, unscrew the expander bolt 2 more turns; lift the wheel off the ground, holding the bike by

Above: Note the minimum insertion depth marking on the stem.

Below: Opening the stem collar by tightening the spreader screw.

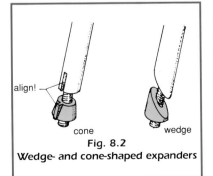

align!

cone   wedge

Fig. 8.2
Wedge- and cone-shaped expanders

the handlebars, then tap on the expander bolt with the mallet, after which it will usually come loose. If it doesn't, apply some spray lubricant or penetrating oil between the stem and the collar or locknut at the top of the headset and try again.

4. Remove the handlebars complete with the stem.

Installation Procedure:

1. Clean the stem and the inside of the steerer tube with a clean cloth, then put some grease on the wedge (or the cone) and the part of the stem that will go inside the steerer tube, in order to prevent rust and to ease subsequent adjustment or replacement.

2. Tighten the expander bolt so far that the wedge is correctly aligned and snug up to the stem's slanted end, still allowing free movement of the stem in the steerer tube.

3. If a cone-shape device is used instead of a wedge, align the ribs on the cone with the slots in the end of the stem.

4. Install the stem and position it in the correct orientation, but make sure it is not so high that the maximum height mark engraved on the stem protrudes above the headset locknut, so that the stem is clamped in securely.

5. Straddle the front wheel, keeping it straight relative to the bike's frame, and put the handlebars in the required position as regards height and orientation, holding them steady with one hand.

6. Still holding the handlebars firmly in place, tighten the expander bolt.

7. Verify whether the handlebars are now in the right position, and make any corrections that may be necessary.

8. If the brake's adjustment was affected (see step 1 above), tension the cable and adjust the brake as described in Chapter 5.

Replace Handlebars or Stem Separately

This must be done when the handlebars are seriously damaged or when you want to install another size or model of either the stem or the handlebars. When replacing either, first check whether the handlebars and the stem have matching diameters. Generally, it is easiest to do this without first removing the stem from the bike, so that you can use the bike for leverage.

Tools and equipment:
3–6 mm Allen wrenches (on older bikes, a 12 mm wrench) medium-sized and large screwdrivers

Top: *Removing the handlebars.*

Center: *Taping at brake lever mount.*

Bottom: *Installing the end plug.*

Removal Procedure:

1. Remove any components installed on the handlebars, e.g., handlebar tape or handgrips, brake levers, gear shifters—after first releasing tension in the cables.

2. Loosen and remove the bolt(s) that clamp the stem collar around the handlebars.

3. Using the big screwdriver, spread open the collar and pull the thicker section of the handlebars out of the collar. If the stem has a spreader screw, screw it in to open up the collar until it is open wide enough to clear the handlebars.

4. Twist the handlebars in such a way as to find the most favorable position to release them from the stem.

Installation Procedure:

1. Open up the handlebars as described in step 3 above.

2. Push the handlebars through the collar, twisting if necessary, until the thicker section is reached, then open up the collar with the big screwdriver or, on models with a spreader screw, by screwing it in using the small Allen wrench.

3. Push the handlebars into the correct position.

4. Install the binder bolts and tighten them until the bars are just gripped but not tight.

5. Adjust the handlebars to the exact position desired and hold them there firmly while tightening the bolts. On a model with a spreader screw, remember to slacken it off before attempting to tighten the binder bolts.

6. Install all the components required on the handlebars.

7. Check the position and alignment again, making any adjustments that may be necessary.

8. Finally, on models with a spreader screw, tighten it, so it won't get lost.

Replace Handlebar Tape

Drop handlebars are usually covered with handlebar tape, which has to be replaced when it gets uncomfortable or unsightly due to wear or damage. You will also have to rewrap it if it has been removed in order to replace a brake lever or the stem. Since brake cables are often routed along the bars, you will have to rewrap when replacing an outer cable.

Choose either non-adhesive cork, plastic or cloth tape, or tape with a narrow adhesive backing strip. At least one roll of tape is needed for each side. Most sets of handlebar tape come with two short pre-cut pieces to be used at the brake hoods where the handlebars are bare.

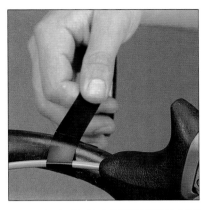

Procedure:

1. Remove the old handlebar tape after loosening the handlebar end plugs. Adhesive tape may have to be cut, after which it is advisable to clean the adhesive off with methyl alcohol. Lift the rubber brake hoods off the levers so that they clear the handlebars, and place the short sections of tape there.

2. Adhesive tape is wound starting from a point about 7.5 cm (3 in.) from the center, working toward the ends. Overlap each layer generously with the preceding one and wrap in an X-pattern around the brake lever attachments.

3. Non-adhesive tape is wound starting from the ends, after tucking a piece inside. Work toward the center, and overlap as described above for adhesive tape. Fasten the ends by wrapping some adhesive tape around them.

4. Install the end plugs, and tighten them with a screwdriver if they are of the variety with an expander screw in the end.

Top: Tape brake or gear cables down in place along the handlebars.

Center: Removal of sticky handgrips.

Bottom: Bar-ends are clamped inside or around the ends of the handlebars. You'll have to cut the ends off the handgrips.

Remove and Replace Handgrips

On a mountain bike or a roadster, you may want to replace the handgrips with a more comfortable type. You will also have to remove them when replacing the bars without the stem.

Tools and equipment:
small screwdriver
cloth
dishwashing liquid
hot water
special adhesive or hairspray

Procedure:

1. Lift the ends of the grips off the handlebars a little with the small screwdriver and introduce some dishwashing liquid if they won't come off easily.

2. Before reinstalling the handgrips, remove all traces of dishwashing liquid, so they won't slide off.

3. To install, dip the handgrips in hot water before forcing them over the handlebars, or use the adhesive that is supplied with some grips—it not only holds them in place once installed, it also helps them slip on when it is first applied.

Bar-Ends

Many mountain bike riders feel the regular mountain bike handlebars too restrictive and decide to install bar-ends—extensions pieces at the ends. Internally clamped models have a wedge and an expander bolt that works just like the device that holds the stem in the steerer tube. Externally clamped models have a split collar just like

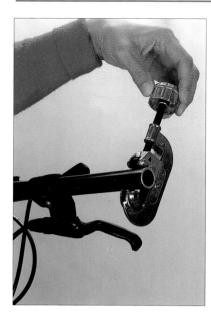

Overly wide mountain bike handlebars can be cut off to the desired width, preferably using a pipe cutter, as shown here. Cut the same length off both ends.

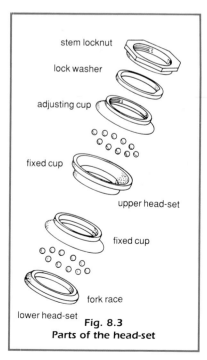

stem locknut

lock washer

adjusting cup

fixed cup

upper head-set

fixed cup

fork race

lower head-set

Fig. 8.3
Parts of the head-set

a handlebar stem. First cut back the ends of the handgrips and then install the bar-ends by tightening the Allen bolt that pulls the wedge inside the handlebar end. You must tighten them firmly enough so that they don't slip under load. Get the size that matches the diameter of your handlebars, and check to make sure your handlebars are strong enough for the use of bar-ends—some of the lightest handlebars are not.

Shorten Straight Handlebars

Some mountain bikes are still supplied with excessively wide handlebars. If you are not unusually big, you may want to shorten them to about 55 cm (22 in.), but certainly to no more than 60 cm (24 in.) total width. This can be done once they are installed, using either a pipe cutter (from a plumbing supply store) or a hacksaw. This changes the bike's handling characteristics, so be careful when riding the bike until you get used to the new situation.

Tools and equipment:
pipe cutter or hacksaw

handlebar tape
file

Procedure:

1. Remove handgrips and measure off the same distance on both sides, marking the location to be cut.

2. If you use a hacksaw, wind some handlebar tape around the bars at the desired cut location to use as a guide to make sure you cut them straight.

3. Stand in such a position that you can cut perfectly square, and preferably get someone else to hold the bike and the handlebars firmly.

4. File the rough edge smooth.

5. Reinstall all components that were removed from the handlebars.

The Headset

The headset forms the link between the steering system and the frame. It consists of two sets of ball bearings installed at either end of the head tube. The lower headset bearing sits between the fork crown and the bottom of the head tube. The upper headset bearing is adjustable, with the adjusting parts screwed onto the top end of the fork's steerer tube. The handlebar stem projects from the locknut at the top of the upper headset bearing.

Although most road bike headsets are made to the same dimensions and are mutually interchangeable, the matter is complicated on mountain bikes. Many of those use an oversize headset. The headset's nominal size is referenced by the outside diameter of the steerer tube. Work on oversize headsets calls for special tools. Use the standard 32 mm tool for the standard 1-in. headset, a 36 mm tool for a 1⅛-in. headset, and a 40 mm tool for a 1¼-in. headset.

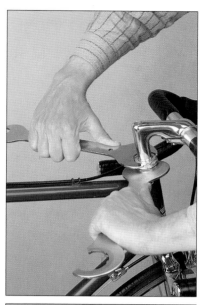

Top: *Adjusting the headset bearing.*
Center: *Removing the locknut.*
Bottom: *Keyed lock washer on the upper headset bearing.*

Adjust Headset

If the steering is rough or loose, first try to solve the problem by adjusting the headset bearings. If this does not do the trick, the bearing cups may well have been damaged—either as a result of impact from the bearing balls or due to overtightening. In that case, you will have to overhaul the headset.

Tools and equipment: headset wrench (or a large adjustable wrench)

Procedure:

1. Loosen the collar or locknut on the upper headset bearing by about one turn if there is no serrated ring under it—enough to free the latter if there is. If there is a worm screw to clamp the locknut down, undo it first.

2. Lift the washer under this nut enough to release the underlying part, which is the adjustable bearing cup.

3. Tighten or loosen the adjustable bearing cup by turning it by about one eighth of a turn in the appropriate direction if the bearing is too loose or too tight. Usually this can be done by hand without a wrench.

4. Hold the adjustable bearing cup perfectly still by facing the bike with the front wheel firmly clamped between your legs and holding the cup with the headset wrench.

5. Put the washer in place and tighten the locknut while restraining the adjustable cup.

6. Check to make sure the adjustment is correct; readjust if necessary, following the same procedure.

7. On models with a worm screw to clamp the locknut down, tighten it, so that the locknut won't come loose accidentally.

Note:
To keep track of your adjustment, it is a good idea to mark the adjustable cup and the head tube with a vertical line, showing the original alignment of the two. Then turn the adjustable cup 6 mm (¼ in.) to the right, clockwise, looking down on it from the top, if you want to tighten the headset (or to the left, counterclockwise, if you want to loosen it).

Overhaul Headset

If adjusting does not solve your problem, the headset bearings must be disassembled, and individual parts cleaned, inspected and lubricated—or, if they are damaged, replaced. The same procedures are followed when either the headset or the fork is replaced. Before doing this work, remove the handlebars with the stem as described in the

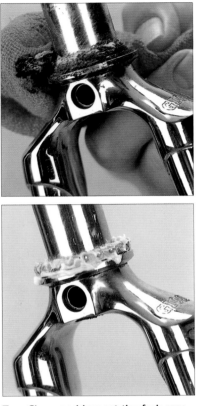

Top: Clean and inspect the fork race and the matching bearing parts.
Center: Grease all bearing parts.
Bottom: Reassemble the headset.

beginning of this chapter. On a bike with cantilever or centerpull brakes, first loosen the front brake cable.

Tools and equipment:

headset wrenches (or large adjustable wrenches)

bearing grease
cloths

Dismantling Procedure:

1. Loosen and remove the collar or locknut on top of the headset (after unscrewing a clamping screw, if installed).

2. Remove the lockwasher by lifting it straight off.

3. Unscrew the adjustable bearing cup, while holding the fork to the frame.

4. Remove the bearing balls, which are usually held in a bearing-ball retainer.

5. Pull the fork out from the frame, also catching the lower bearing balls, again usually held in a retainer. If loose balls are used, make sure you remove all of them and check their size—different diameters are used on different makes and models.

Inspection and Overhauling Procedure:

1. Inspect all parts for wear, corrosion, grooves, and pitting. Irregular pitting of the bearing races, referred to as brinelling and caused by axial impact, is particularly pernicious. This problem is often caused or aggravated by improper adjustment—that's why it pays to check and adjust the headset bearings once a month.

2. Replace the entire headset if significant damage is apparent in the cups. Always replace the bearing balls, making sure to count them and buy the correct size, either individually or in a retainer.

3. If the headset bearing races have to be replaced, get the old fixed cups and the fork-crown race removed, and new ones installed, with special tools at a bike shop.

Installation Procedure:

1. If the fixed cups and the fork race are serviceable, or once they have been replaced, fill the bearing cups with bearing grease.

2. Hold the frame upside down and embed one of the bearing retainers, or a set of loose bearings, in the grease-filled lower fixed bearing race (which is now facing up). The retainer must be installed in such a way that the bearing balls—not the metal ring—contact the inside of the cup.

Top: *Install the adjustable cup.*
Center: *Install the locknut.*
Bottom: *Tighten the locknut while restraining the adjustable cup.*

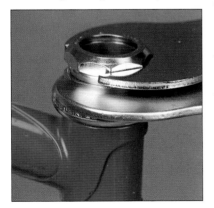

3. Hold the fork upside-down and put it through the head tube.

4. Turn the frame the right way round again.

5. Embed the other bearing retainer, or loose bearings, in the grease-filled upper fixed bearing cup.

6. Screw the adjustable bearing cup onto the threaded end of the fork's steerer tube by hand.

7. Place the keyed lock washer on top of the adjustable cup with the flat part matching the flat part of the fork's steerer tube, and do the same with any part that may have been installed to serve as a brake cable anchor.

8. Screw the collar or locknut onto the threaded end of the steerer tube, without tightening it completely.

9. Install the front wheel.

10. Adjust the bearings as outlined in the previous description *Adjust Headset*. Take your time for this adjustment, because it can ruin your headset (and impair the bike's handling) if it is too tight or too loose.

11. Center and adjust the stem with the handlebars, and readjust the brake cable if necessary.

12. On models with a clamping screw, screw it in to clamp the locknut tight.

The Front Fork

Forks come in many different sizes, and some have French or Italian threading, even if they appear to have the standard diameter. The length of the steerer tube has to match the bike's head tube, and the fork blades have to match the wheel size.

If the steering gets sticky when turning the bars, even though it seems fine when going straight, it will be due to a bent steerer tube, usually as a result of a collision. When replacing a fork that is bent, make sure the bosses installed for the brakes are in the right location for the kind of brakes used, and check the length of the steerer tube, which must also be the same as the old one—assuming it was correct. You can establish the correct length by adding the stacking height of the headset (given by the headset manufacturer) to the length of the head tube and deducting 2 mm ($3/32$ in.).

Inspect and Replace Front Fork

This will be necessary whenever you have had a serious crash or when the bike does not seem to steer the way it should. Generally, a visual check is adequate for the typical kinds of damage possible.

Although it may sometimes be possible to straighten a bent fork, I suggest you replace the entire fork. This will give you a sorely needed margin of safety that may prevent a bad crash later on. Sometimes the fork's steerer tube has to be cut shorter to fit the frame. It is

Top: Removing the fork from the head tube.
Center: One kind of fork damage: bent brake pivot boss on a mountain bike fork.
Bottom: Removal and installation of the crown race (and the fixed races) requires special tools.

preferable to get that done at the bike shop, since the thread often has to be recut too.

If you decide to do it yourself, screw the locknut on as a guide so you'll cut straight. Be careful not to cut it too short—better to add an extra washer or file it down further than ruin your fork. File any burrs off the end before installing the fork. Before doing this work, remove the handlebars with the stem. On a bike with a cantilever or centerpull brake in the front, loosen the brake cable and remove the front wheel.

Tools and equipment:
3–6 mm Allen wrenches

headset wrenches or large adjustable wrenches

Procedure:

1. Release the front brake cable and remove the entire front brake; then remove the front wheel.

2. Remove the handlebars with the stem.

3. Dismantle the upper headset as outlined in *Overhaul Headset.*

4. Remove the fork, following the same description.

5. Take the old fork to the bike shop as a reference when buying the new one.

6. Install the fork and reassemble the headset as described under *Overhaul Headset.*

7. Install the handlebars as described above.

8. Install the front brake and hook up the cable.

9. Install the front wheel.

10. Check and adjust all parts affected: headset, stem, handlebars, front brake.

Suspension Fork Installation and Maintenance

In recent years, telescoping front forks have become popular for mountain bikes. The number of different versions on the market is too great to do justice to any one of the detailed maintenance instructions.

Perhaps the most important advice is to keep them scrupulously clean, especially near the area where the thinner section telescopes into the thicker section. Any dirt that penetrates is likely to reach the seals (on models with hydraulic dampers) and cause leakage, resulting in inadequate damping. On models without hydraulic damping, penetrating dirt may cause the parts to bind up, resulting in unpredictable behavior.

Regularly check for any apparent looseness or tightness in the suspension and steering functions. If you notice a loss of front end control when riding, that will probably be owing to damage to the fork's mechanism. Refer any work that goes beyond cleaning and adjusting to a bike mechanic familiar with this kind of equipment.

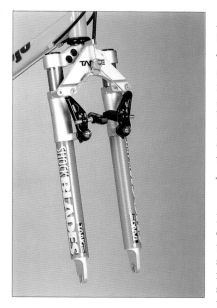

Above: Typical telescoping mountain bike suspension fork. Note the bridge piece connecting the two slider tubes at the brake bosses, which is needed to keep the fork blades parallel.

Below: On an elastomer-damped suspension fork, you can usually disassemble the struts to replace the pads with stiffer or softer ones.

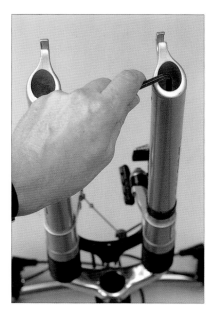

Alternatively, you can request the specific maintenance instructions from the manufacturer of the fork.

To install a suspension fork, follow the same procedure as previously described for a rigid fork. When selecting one as a replacement for a rigid fork, make sure you select one with the same steerer tube diameter and length. That's easiest to do when you take the whole bike to the shop so it can be measured by an expert. Once installed, take the bike for a test ride. If the steering feels loose, check over the entire installation again. If you can't figure out yourself what is wrong, take it to the bike shop.

Elastomer Suspension Fork Maintenance

Most suspension forks have a knob or a dial with which the frictional damping is adjusted. They can be dismantled to replace the elastomer pads. Always keep your adjustments symmetrical, so that both sides of the fork are adjusted the same way. Generally, heavier riders need stiffer pads and more damping than do light riders. If the suspension seems too soft, turn the dial clockwise to tighten up on the friction damping; turn counterclockwise to loosen it up. Try out various settings to establish which way seems most comfortable, and proceed to changing the elastomer pads only if adjustment does not have the desired effect.

To replace the elastomer pads, first take the front wheel out and dismantle the fork blade, which on most models is done from a large screw cap at the top. Take the inner sliding tube out to reveal something that looks like a plunger that is mounted between elastomer pads. The pads will be color-coded according to their firmness. Generally the stiffest are white, moderately firm ones are yellow, and the softest ones are red. Select the combination that seems right, considering your weight, riding style and the feel of the forks before modification. It is possible to mix and match, in which case the stiffest ones are used at the ends, the softest ones in the middle. Finally, reassemble the fork and test-ride it immediately—and make such additional adjustments as may seem appropriate.

Air-Sprung Suspension Fork Maintenance

Of all the "shocks" on the market, this type, of which the Rock-Shox is the best-known example, is technically the most sophisticated, and consequently also the most sensitive. The pressure is adjusted by changing the gas pressure (either nitrogen or simply air, depending on the make and model in question). Most of the models that use air can be controlled via a simple valve (either like that on a car tire or like the one on a football), using a pump or a compressor with the matching adaptor. The tension is lowered by letting off some air by pushing in the valve pin. Heavy riders, rough terrain and high speeds require higher pressures than lighter riders, less rugged terrain and lower speeds.

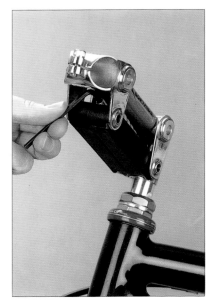

This flexible stem provides excellent shock-absorption and is easy to install, even on a bike that was not designed with suspension in mind. It relies on a coil spring, which can be pre-tensioned as shown to increase the stiffness.

These forks use compressed air as a spring, and their movement is damped by means of a hydraulic shock absorber—a piston with a small hole moving up and down in an oil-filled cylinder. Within the normal range, damping is increased by selecting a higher number, and decreased by selecting a lower number on the dial. If damping is still inadequate, you may replace the oil by a type with a higher viscosity. Although the manufacturers offer proprietary brands, you can use automatic transmission fluid (ATF), available from auto parts shops. This is available in several viscosity grades—the higher the number the stiffer will be the damping effect.

Other Front Suspension Types

The simplest form of effective suspension is by means of a sprung stem, of which there are several types on the market. In most cases, a coil spring is used, supplemented by elastomer pads to soften the bottoming out. On cheaper models, only an elastomer pad is used as a spring. The most sophisticated coil-spring models have an adjuster to vary the preload effect on the coil spring: the more preload, the stiffer the suspension with respect to small unevennesses. In addition, there may be a friction adjustment to increase or decrease the damping effect.

Since this kind of suspension does not affect the steering geometry, as all suspension forks do, it can be retrofitted by the home mechanic to any existing bike—it does not even have to be a mountain bike. Simply follow the instructions for removal and installation of the handlebars and the stem elsewhere in this chapter.

CHAPTER 9

The Frame

ALTHOUGH the frame is the bicycle's major single part, it is fortunately rarely in need of maintenance or repair work. And when something does happen, it is likely to be so serious that the average rider decides to call it a day and perhaps even retire the bike. Just the same, there are some maintenance aspects of the frame that will be covered here.

Above: The bicycle frame. This is the most conventional type of road bike frame with lugged joints.

Below: More and more specialist bikes reach the market, and many of them need a non-standard frame, such as this model with rear suspension.

Frame Construction

The front part, or main frame, is made up of large-diameter tubes. These are called the top tube, down tube, seat tube and head tube. The bottom bracket shell is at the frame's lowest point. The rear triangle is built up of double sets of smaller-diameter tubes, called seat stays and chain stays. Each pair is connected by means of a short bridge piece.

Traditionally, bike frames are constructed with external lugs and brazed-in tubes. More recently many frames have been built without lugs, and the tubes may be either welded, bonded or brazed together. The tubes of brazed frames are always of steel, whereas the other methods may be used with more exotic tubing materials, such as aluminum, titanium and carbon-fiber.

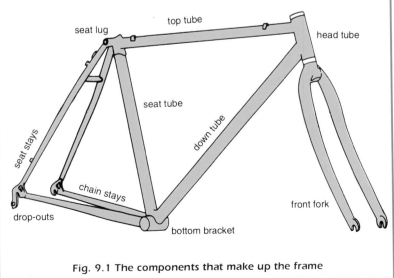

Fig. 9.1 The components that make up the frame

Two types of frame joint: lugged (above) and lugless (below). The latter method is used for many mountain bikes, either TIG-welded or fillet-brazed.

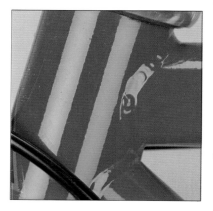

Whether welded, brazed or bonded, one lug is always present: the seat lug. It is split in the back and clamped together to hold the seatpost. At the ends where the stays meet there are flat plates, called drop-outs, in which the wheel is installed. The one on the right also contains a threaded eye, to which the derailleur is mounted. Finally, there are a number of small parts, referred to as braze-ons. These include the mounting bosses for downtube-mounted shift levers on road bikes; pivot bosses for the cantilever brakes used on mountain, hybrid or touring bikes; little bosses for the installation of water bottle and luggage rack; and guides for the control cables.

Frame Damage

In the case of a head-on collision, there is a chance of the down tube literally buckling at a point just behind the head tube. Left unchecked, this will eventually lead to the frame's collapse, which may prove highly dangerous. It's the kind of damage only a professional frame builder can solve for you—and one that's only worthwhile on an expensive frame, because the down tube has to be removed and replaced by a new one.

Other kinds of frame damage are less dramatic, though they may be serious enough. A collision, a fall or other forms of abuse may cause the frame to get out of alignment. You can verify this from time to time by trying to line up front and rear wheels while looking from behind. If it can't be done, either the frame or the front fork is misaligned. The descriptions below show you how to check the frame and what to do about it. Finally, it sometimes happens that one of the drop-outs gets bent. Instructions to establish and correct this problem are also included below.

The possibilities of aligning and bending are limited to conventional steel frames. Don't try this kind of operation on frames made of aluminum, nor on the lightest varieties of steel (such as Reynolds 753, Columbus SL, or Tange Prestige tubing). As for composite and bonded frames, they just can't be bent or straightened, not even by an experienced bike mechanic or frame builder.

Frame Alignment Check

In this and the following procedures, all the checks that can be carried out relatively simply will be described in some detail. Always see a bike shop about correcting any damage detected.

Tools and equipment: 3 m (10 ft.) of twine
                                  ruler marked in mm or 32nds

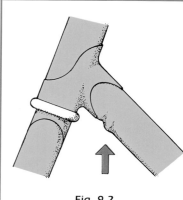

Fig. 9.2
Typical frame tube damage

Procedure:

1. Remove the rear wheel from the bike, following the relevant description in Chapter 7.

2. Wrap the twine around the frame, pulling it taut at the drop-outs.

Top: Typical RH drop-out on a high-quality steel frame.
Center: Bottom bracket detail on a lugged frame.

Bottom left and right: Frame alignment check: compare the distance between the tube and the string on both sides.

3. Measure the distance between the twine and the seat tube on both sides. If they are not identical (plus or minus perhaps 1 or 2 mm at the most), let a bike mechanic determine whether the frame can be straightened—it's not the kind of job to do yourself.

Drop-out Check

After a fall, the reason for derailleur problems may be that the rear derailleur eye (on the RH rear drop-out) is bent. In other cases, the wheel won't center, even though it seems to be undamaged (as checked in Chapter 7). To establish whether the drop-outs are still straight after a fall or rough transportation, proceed as follows.

Tools and equipment: 60 cm (2 ft.) metal straightedge

Procedure:

1. Remove the rear wheel from the bike, following the relevant procedure in Chapter 7.

2. Hold the straightedge snug up against the outside of the drop-outs on both sides, holding, but not forcing, the other end near the down tube.

3. Measure and compare the distance between the straightedge and the seat tube on both sides.

4. Measure the distance between the drop-outs and compare it with the sum of the seat tube diameter and the two distances measured in step 3.

5. If the difference is more than 3 mm (⅛ in.), at least one of the drop-outs should be straightened—preferably by a bike mechanic.

Top: Typical investment-cast brake bridge between the rear stays of a high-quality road bike.

Center: Detail of front derailleur lug brazed onto the seat tube on a modern road bike.

Bottom: Touching up chipped paint.

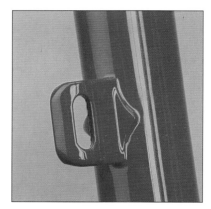

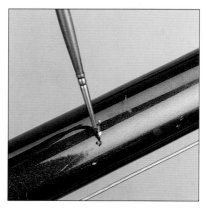

Usually, you can tell which one is bent.

Note:
Any misalignment noticed in this test should not be corrected by the home mechanic. Consult a competent bike mechanic or a frame builder to correct the problem.

Paint Damage Touch-up

However careful you are, you can't help but scratch up your bike sometimes. At least once a year it will be worthwhile to touch up any nicks and scratches.

Tools and equipment:
touch-up paint
fine-tip paint brush
cloth
fine sandpaper
paint thinner

Procedure:

1. Clean the bike thoroughly to uncover any places that may have to be touched up.

2. Sand down the area of the damage, folding the sandpaper into a tiny pad.

3. Clean the area with a dry cloth.

4. Dip the brush in the paint very sparingly, and treat only the area where the paint has been removed, minimizing any overlapping of paint that is still intact.

5. Clean the brush in paint thinner immediately after use and let it dry suspended with the bristles down but not touching anything.

6. Allow the paint to dry at least overnight before touching the frame again.

Note:

If you can get paint only in a spraycan, spray a little in a bottle cap and dip the brush in it. Once you have finished, hold the spraycan upside down and spray until clean air—not paint—comes out of the nozzle, so the spraycan will work the next time you need it.

CHAPTER 10

Saddle and Seatpost

General view of saddle and seatpost on a modern mountain bike with a quick-release binder bolt.

WHILE these are not amongst the most trouble-prone components on the modern bicycle, they do justify some attention. The jobs described here will be adjustment of the position of the saddle (also called seat), replacement of saddle and seatpost and any maintenance needed on a leather saddle. The Hite-Rite adjusting aid, installed on many top-quality mountain bikes, is described in Chapter 11, which deals with accessories.

On mountain bikes, the binder bolt usually takes the form of a quick-release mechanism. The saddle position should be adjusted whenever the bike is set up for another rider or when the position is uncomfortably high or low.

Adjust Saddle Height

In this and the following descriptions, we shall merely explain how the actual adjustment operations are carried out, assuming you know how high you want the saddle to be.

Tools and Equipment:

3–5 mm Allen wrench	grease
6-in. adjustable wrench	cloth

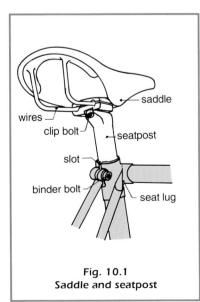

Fig. 10.1
Saddle and seatpost

(labels: saddle, wires, clip bolt, seatpost, slot, binder bolt, seat lug)

Procedure:

1. Undo the binder bolt, or on a mountain bike, flip the lever of the quick-release binder bolt to the open position in order to loosen the seatpost.

2. The seatpost, with the saddle still attached, should now be free to move up and down. If it is not, undo the bolt further, or on a mountain bike hold the QR lever and unscrew the thumb nut on the other side by about one turn. If it still isn't free, apply some penetrating oil between the seatpost and the seat lug, wait a minute or two and try again, if necessary using the saddle to twist the seatpost relative to the frame.

3. Place the saddle in the desired position. If penetrating oil was needed, first remove the seatpost, then clean the seatpost and the interior of the seat tube and apply some grease to the outside of the seatpost.

Above: To adjust the seat height or to remove the seatpost, loosen the binder bolt in the back of the seat lug.

Below: Detail of the seat lug, showing the binder bolt on a typical modern road bike frame.

4. Hold the saddle at the correct height, and align it perfectly straight forward. Tighten the binder bolt or flip the quick-release lever to the closed position.

5. On a model with quick-release, check whether the saddle is now installed firmly. If not, loosen the quick-release lever, tighten the thumb nut perhaps one turn, and try again.

6. Try out and readjust if necessary until the position is satisfactory.

Note:
If you have a mountain bike with a Hite-Rite spring adjuster, apply just enough downward force on the saddle to achieve the desired position when adjusting. If the range of the Hite-Rite is incorrect for the required saddle position, undo the clamp around the seatpost and attach it higher or lower as required. Refer to Chapter 11 for additional details.

Adjust Saddle Angle and Position

Generally, both of these adjustments are carried out with the bolts that hold the saddle to the seatpost. These can be reached from under the saddle, except on some special seatposts.

Tools and equipment: 3–5 mm Allen wrench
6-in. adjustable wrench

Procedure:

1. If the saddle must be moved forward or backward, loosen both bolts by about one or two turns each.

2. Holding the clamp on top of the seatpost with one hand and the saddle with the other, move the latter to the correct position.

3. If the saddle has to be merely tipped, the front raised or lowered relative to the rear portion, loosen the nuts, and then move the saddle as required.

4. Holding the saddle in the correct position, tighten the bolts, making sure it does not move while doing so.

5. Check and readjust if necessary.

Replace Saddle and Seatpost

It is usually easier to remove the combination of saddle and seatpost than to remove the saddle alone. This is also the first step in removing the seatpost.

Tools and Equipment: 6-in. adjustable wrench
3–5 mm Allen wrench

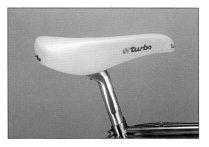

Top: Adjusting the tilt of the saddle.

Center: In the normal position, the top of the saddle is horizontal.

Bottom: Some seatposts have an additional tilt adjustment screw.

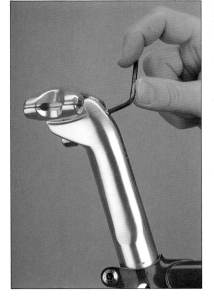

Removal Procedure:

1. Loosen the binder bolt or the quick-release lever until the seatpost can be moved up or down freely, as described under *Adjust Saddle Height.*

2. Pull out the seatpost with the saddle.

Installation Procedure:

1. Clean the outside of the seatpost and the inside of the seat tube, then smear grease on the seatpost to prevent corrosion and to ease subsequent adjustments.

2. Install the seatpost with the saddle fitted and adjust it to the correct height.

3. If you are installing the seatpost with a Hite-Rite, clamp it around the seatpost when it is perfectly aligned and at the maximum height you want the saddle to be.

4. Tighten the quick-release binder bolt as described under *Adjust Saddle Height.*

Note:
If your bike has a conventional tubular two-piece seatpost, the adjusting mechanism will be contained in a separate clip that connects the saddle to the seatpost by means of a bolt with a nut on each end. Usually, only one of the nuts needs to be loosened, keeping the one on the other side in place.

Maintenance of Leather Saddle

If you use a real leather saddle (as opposed to the usual nylon one with a thin leather cover), make sure it does not get wet. Wrap a plastic bag around the saddle when transporting the bike or leaving it outside when there is the slightest chance of rain. If it does get wet, don't sit on it until it is thoroughly dried out, since otherwise it will deform permanently. To keep it water resistant and slightly flexible, treat it with leather treatment such as Brooks Proofide at least twice a year.

Adjust the tension of a leather saddle no more than once a year and only when it is noticeably sagged, tightening the tensioning bolt with the saddle manufacturer's special wrench (regular wrenches don't fit in such a tight spot)—perhaps one turn at the most. Don't overdo this adjustment, since it often causes the saddle to be pulled into an uncomfortable shape.

Even for a sagging cover there is a cure. Drill 4 holes near the middle of each side of the cover, about 8 mm ($5/16$ in.), and then tie the two sides up underneath the saddle the way you might tie your shoelaces. Distribute the tension in such a way that the saddle cover's shape comes as close as possible to the original shape.

109

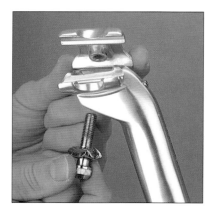 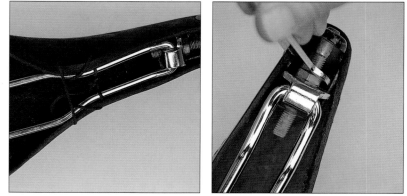

Left: High-end adjustable seatpost dismantled.

Center: A stretched leather saddle can sometimes be saved by tying it this way.

Right: The leather saddle cover's tension can be adjusted with the nut on the tensioning bolt.

Install Sprung Leather Saddle

The most comfortable leather saddles, such as the Brooks ATB Conquest, have double wires and coil springs. To fit this kind of saddle on an adjustable seatpost, you will have to either install the matching model or use a special adaptor between the wires in the saddle. Place the adaptor on the saddle's two pairs of wires and between the seatpost's main part and its clamp, then tighten the bolts and adjust the saddle as described elsewhere in this chapter.

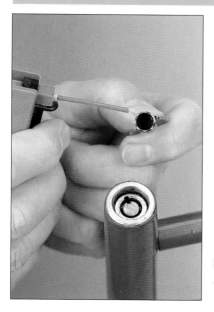

CHAPTER 11

Accessories

MOST cyclists like to keep their bikes as light as possible. However, accessories can extend the usefulness of any bike. In fact, several accessories are commonly installed on specific models, especially commuter bikes, and they can be added to most bikes if you wish. This chapter will briefly describe how to install and maintain the most useful accessories. We'll cover the following:

- ☐ pump
- ☐ seat adjuster
- ☐ toeclips
- ☐ lighting equipment
- ☐ luggage racks

- ☐ fenders
- ☐ chainguard
- ☐ kick stand
- ☐ bicycle computer

Above: The U-lock can be mounted on a bracket attached to a frame tube. To maintain it, all you need to do is put some oil on the key and then lock and unlock it a few times.

Below: With bells and whistles: Left: Heavily accessorized city-type mountain bikes.

Right: Typical Dutch utility bike with lots of protective equipment.

The Pump

At home, a big stand pump with hose connector and an integrated pressure gauge is most useful for fast and controlled tire inflation. On the bike, you will need a smaller model. In addition to the standard versions intended for road bikes, there are special mountain bike pumps available. These have a larger diameter than the models intended for road bikes, allowing you to pump more air with each stroke of the pump, though at a slightly lower pressure. Recently, CO_2-gas inflators have become popular, but they are more hassle than they are worth. Whatever type you use, get a pump with the kind of head or hose connector to match the valves on your bike's tires. If you have to maintain bikes with different types of valves, buy an adaptor nipple to convert from one to the other.

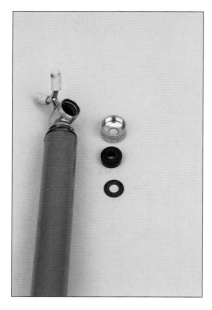

Above: Even the pump can be serviced: parts of the head.

Pump Maintenance

If the pump doesn't work properly, the leak is usually at the head of the pump (the part that is put on the valve) or at the plunger inside the pump. On some pumps, the head can be replaced.

Tools and equipment: screwdriver
                                  lubricant

Procedure:

1. Tighten the screwed bushing that holds down the rubber sealing washer, or grommet, in the head of the pump.

2. If this doesn't solve the problem, unscrew it and check the grommet, replacing it if necessary (inflexible, cut, frayed or enlarged hole); then screw the bushing back on.

3. If still no luck, unscrew the other end of the pump and check the condition of the leather or plastic plunger washer. If it is no longer flexible, impregnate it with any kind of vegetable or animal fat and make sure it is screwed down tight. If necessary, replace the plunger washer.

Install and Remove Seat Adjuster (Hite-Rite)

For off-road riding, the Hite-Rite is a useful device for mountain bikes that allows you to adjust your seat while riding the bike.

Tools and Equipment: 6 mm adjustable wrench
                                  screwdriver

Below: One end of the Hite-Rite is clamped around the seat's quick-release binder bolt and the other around the seatpost.

Installation Procedure:

1. Place the Hite-Rite's lower clip in position at the seat lug's eye bolt.

2. Install the quick-release binder bolt, holding the Hite-Rite in the correct position with the eye between the seat lug eye and the thumbnut.

3. Loosely install the seatpost with the saddle.

4. Tighten the Hite-Rite clamp around the seatpost when the seat is as high as you'll ever want it to be.

5. Complete installation and adjustment of the seatpost and the saddle.

6. Check to make sure the seatpost can be adjusted over the desired range and make any corrections necessary.

Above: Install the headlight—whether it is battery- or generator-powered—as high as practicable and aim it at the road about 20–30 ft. (6–10 m) ahead of the bike.

Below: One of the best and brightest lights available—the Night Rider, with high and low beam, and a central battery in a pouch or a water bottle.

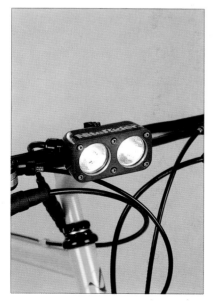

Removal Procedure:

1. Loosen the clamp that holds the Hite-Rite around the seatpost.

2. Remove the saddle with the seatpost.

3. Remove the quick-release binder bolt, by unscrewing the thumbnut all the way.

4. Pull the Hite-Rite off the seat lug's eye bolt.

Toeclips

Toeclips are the traditinal way to secure the feet on the pedals. With the advent of clipless pedals, toeclips are being edged out of the road bike market, but still have the advantage that you can ride your bike with the same shoes you use for walking. In addition to the conventional toeclips with a strap wrapped around the shoe, there are short metal or plastic strapless clips. All models are installed on the pedal with a set of small screws with nuts to lock them in place. The strap should be twisted where it passes through the pedal to prevent it from slipping.

Lighting Equipment

For nighttime riding on city streets, almost any light will do. However, under off-road conditions, only very expensive high-powered units such as Night Sun and Night Rider seem to be bright enough. For cycling on city streets and on most rural roads and well-surfaced paths, relatively cheap, simple lights are adequate.

Although all the brightest lights rely on separate rechargeable batteries, most of the simplest acceptable lights are powered by either 4 AA-cells or 2 C-cells; however, my preference is for the ones thatrequire two D-cells (the large cylindrical ones), because these allow the use of a brighter bulb and give more hours of output.

Install Battery Lights

This has to be very general advice, since there are so many makes and models, all differing in detail.

Tools and equipment:
6 mm crescent wrench

3–5 mm Allen wrenches
small screwdriver

Procedure:

Get the appropriate mounting hardware and install the lights in such a way that they do not protrude beyond the bike more than necessary. The highest mounting position is generally the best, since it throws fewer confusing shadows and is more readily visible to others.

A really big reflector mounted rather low is at least as visible as even the best rear light to all other road users who have lighting themselves and who could endanger you from behind.

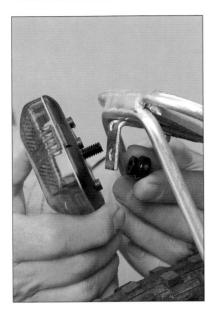

Above: A good place for the rear light or reflector is directly below the back of a luggage rack.

Below: Rapidly flashing LED rear lights are remarkably visible and their batteries last much longer than those of constantly burning lights. For a bike without a luggage rack or a reflector mounting bracket, this is a convenient way to install it.

Battery Light Maintenance

This too has to be very general advice, but is universally valid for all battery systems.

Tools and equipment:

spare batteries
spare bulb

sandpaper
battery terminal grease

Procedure:

1. Usually, when a battery light lets you down, it's a matter of a dead or dying battery. Always check that first by trying the light with other batteries installed.

2. If that does not solve the problem, check whether the bulb is screwed in and firmly contacts the terminal. Scrape the contacts of bulb, battery and terminal to remove dirt or corrosion.

3. If still no luck, check the bulb and replace it if the filament is broken.

4. To prevent corrosion of the contacts, use battery terminal grease to lightly coat the contacts of battery, bulb, switch, and any other parts that carry electricity.

Batteries

The batteries are a special problem for all forms of battery lighting. The most general advice is to keep them dry and preferably warm, and to keep their contacts free from dirt and corrosion, using steel wool and battery terminal grease. Normal dry-cell batteries have an output characteristic that is highly life-dependent: when new, the output is about 1.5 V (Volt) per cell, which gradually falls to an average of 1.2 V, eventually dwindling to nothing. Consequently, the light is bright at first, settles at an average value for some time and then drops off further.

The output of a new battery provides a light that is twice as bright as the average value, while in the end it gives off only a tiny fraction of the average. Bulbs are rated to give their nominal output at the average value of 1.2 V per cell (thus, a bulb for a two-cell unit should be rated at 2.4 V, rather than at 3 V, as would be suggested by the fact that the cells are quoted as providing 1.5 V each).

Rechargeable batteries are available in the form of nickel-cadmium (NiCad) cells (sometimes interchangeable with regular dry cells), or as lead-acid gel batteries suitable only for separate mounting. Both models have entirely different characteristics.

The output of a NiCad cell stays relatively constant at 1.2 V and the light remains almost equally bright up to the (shorter) overall charge life, but suddenly dims without warning. This is one reason to carry fully charged spares if you use NiCads. They also have a limited shelf life and should be depleted and recharged at least once a month—and

discarded when they fail to hold their charge for a week. They do tend to last longer and hold their charge better if drained fully before recharging.

Lead-acid gel type batteries are not available in sizes and shapes that are interchangeable with regular dry cells. They do hold more charge and can be recharged before they are fully run down—in fact, they should never be completely discharged. Consequently, I prefer this type as a central battery wired up to separate light units.

Dynamo Lighting

Dynamo, or generator, lights have the advantage that they are always available for instant use, even if you did not anticipate needing a light—if you give them the little maintenance they need. If they don't work, a systematic approach will usually bring them back to life in little time.

Dynamo Lighting Repair

Bottom-bracket generator. This type runs off the center of the tire and causes less wear and resistance. You may have to keep it tensioned with a bungee cord to prevent slip.

When a dynamo system fails, it is only possible to establish what went wrong if you follow a very systematic approach. After all, this system comprises a large number of mutually connected components. But don't let system rule over logic. Ask yourself what is the most likely cause under the given circumstances. Thus, when it

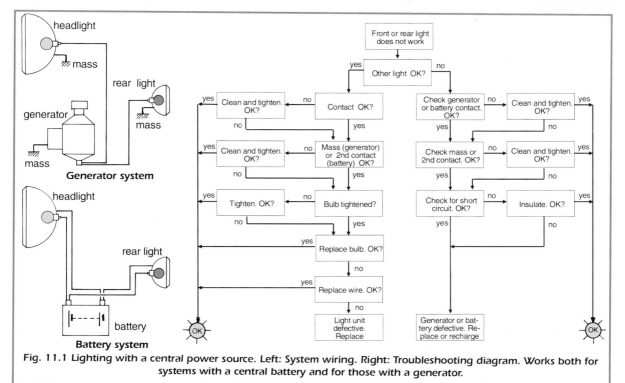

Fig. 11.1 Lighting with a central power source. Left: System wiring. Right: Troubleshooting diagram. Works both for systems with a central battery and for those with a generator.

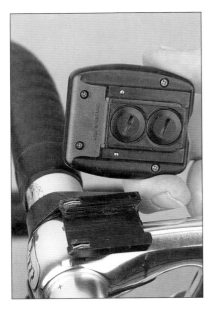

Above: Installing a bicycle computer. Make sure the contacts on the instrument and the mounting clip are clean.

Below: Attachment of luggage rack stays to the rear drop-outs.

is raining or snowing, dynamo slip is more likely to be the cause than in dry weather, so that is the point to start: make sure the dynamo is aligned properly and increase contact pressure by bending the attachment to bring it closer to the tire.

Reflectors

There are a few points to consider in the selection and maintenance of reflectors. In the first place, bigger is better: larger reflectors are more visible than smaller ones, all else being equal. Secondly, lighter-colored reflectors are more visible than darker ones. Amber reflects about twice as much light as red.

As for maintenance, reflectors only do their job properly when they are kept clean: wash them regularly with plenty of water. However, if water should leak inside the reflector, it condenses on the inside, making the reflector virtually blind. For this reason, a cracked or broken reflector should be replaced immediately. To check a reflector's operation, aim a light at it from a distance of 10 m (33 ft.), observing from a point close to the light source whether the reflector appears to light up brightly.

Luggage Racks

The granddaddy of all modern luggage racks is Jim Blackburn's welded aluminum model, and this is still the favorite of many riders, even if the competition offers significantly cheaper racks that look quite similar. Some specialty manufacturers offer welded tubular steel models which are both lighter and sturdier—but at a price.

In the front, use only the so-called low-rider variety, which allows luggage to be carried where it least interferes with steering and bike handling—centered on the steering axis, just behind the front wheel axle. Unfortunately, they do make it hard to transport the bike on most car roof racks.

Luggage Rack Installation

Generally, all luggage racks are attached to bosses welded or brazed onto the bike's frame and front fork.

If your bike does not have the requisite bosses, a clip can be used, providing you first wrap the frame or fork tube where you will mount this clip with a large rubber patch, stuck down with rubber solution just as you would do for a flat tire. This protects the paint and prevents slipping of the clip under the effect of load and vibrations.

Fenders

Generally, fenders are not used on road and mountain bikes in America. However, if you ride in rainy weather or on wet roads or trails, they are essential. Several models are available, the widest and the longest ones being the most effective. Short clip-on guards don't

usually do the trick. In very heavy mud, especially on mountain bikes with limited wheel clearances, fenders can be more trouble than they are worth, since the mud builds up between wheel and fender, soon rendering the former nearly immobile.

Install Fenders

Fenders are installed with stays that connect them to eyelets at the drop-outs and with clips that are bolted to the fork crown (in the front) or to the bridge pieces that connect the chain stays and the seat stays. If you want to make the fenders easily removable, use home-made wing-bolts, made by soldering a washer in the (widened) saw cut of a slotted-head screw.

The stays are clamped in at the fender's metal clips by means of eye bolts. To adjust the position of the fenders, clamp the stays at a different point. Cut off any excess length of the stays, so there are no dangerous protrusions on the bike. If the stays are installed inside the clips, as required in some markets as a safety feature, they must be cut to the right length before installation.

From top to bottom: Attachment of luggage rack to seat stays, of fender stay to fender clip, and of fender to fork crown.

Chainguard

Many roadsters are equipped with a protective guard around the chain, which on some models covers the entire drivetrain. After some use, they tend to bend and twist and then rub against the chain, the crank or the chainrings. Don't just try to twist it while on the bike, because that never seems to have the desired result. Instead, first establish which part needs to be bent which way, then remove it from the bike and bend the attachment clips as appropriate. Check and tighten the attachment bolts once a month.

Kickstand

This device is usually only used on simple bicycles. Although few are any good, some models work better than others. The Japanese model that is attached on the rear stays close to the rear wheel axle is much more effective than the more common type that is attached just behind the bottom bracket.

Another interesting model is the two-legged version. Its advantage is that the bicycle can be balanced on it so that it does not lean over. With this model, either the rear wheel or the front wheel can be raised off the ground to work on the bike. The same maintenance purpose can be achieved by means of a $20 display stand— nothing to install on the bike, but very handy to have at home.

Bicycle Computer

Today, this is about the most common bicycle accessory. Select one that has the minimum number of knobs consistent with the functions you desire. It pays to look for a model that is advertised as being

Check all accessory attachments from time to time.

waterproof and comes with a guarantee to back up this claim. If it is not, put a plastic bag over it in the rain and always take the computer off the bike when transporting it.

Follow the manufacturer's instructions for installation, calibration and maintenance. Generally, it must be calibrated for the wheel size, measured accurately between the road and the wheel axle of the loaded bike.

General Accessory Installation and Maintenance

The following simple rules will help you keep any other accessories on the bike in working order—or at least will prevent their interference with safe operation of the bike.

☐ Attachment must be at a minimum of two points, preferably off-set relative to one another.

☐ If it comes loose, don't just retighten it, but find a better attachment method.

☐ If it gets damaged, remove, repair or replace it immediately.

☐ If it is a moving part, check whether it moves freely without resistance, and lubricate or adjust if not.

TROUBLESHOOTING GUIDE

Problem or Symptom	Possible Cause	Required Correction	See Page
Tiring riding position	1. Incorrect saddle adjustment	Adjust saddle	107, 108
	2. Incorrect handlebar adjustment	Adjust handlebars	91
	3. Incorrect stem extension	Replace stem	93
	4. Incorrect frame size	Replace bike or frame	N/A
High resistance while coasting or pedaling	1. Tire rubs on frame or accessory	Adjust or straighten wheel	77
	2. Wheel bearings worn or tight	Adjust and lubricate	81
	3. Insufficient tire pressure	Inflate tire	27, 90
High resistance while pedaling only	1. Chain dirty, worn or dry	Clean, lubricate, or replace	71
	2. Bottom bracket bearings out of adjustment	Adjust, lubricate, overhaul, or replace	65
	3. Pedal bearings out of adjustment	Adjust, lubricate, or replace	69
	4. Chain or chainring rubs on frame	Straighten or replace, correct chain line	67, 71, 73
Rubbing or scraping sounds while pedaling or coasting	1. See above (as for *High resistance while pedaling*)	See above	
Bike pulls to one side	1. Wheels misaligned	Adjust, center, and align	77, 83
	2. Front fork bent	Replace or straighten	99
	3. Headset damaged	Overhaul or replace	97
	4. Frame out of alignment	Straighten or replace	104
Bike vibrates at high speed	1. Wheels misaligned	Adjust or align	77, 83
	2. Wheel bearings loose	Adjust	81
	3. Headset out of adjustment	Adjust, overhaul, or replace	97
Disturbing noises while pedaling	1. Chainring, crank or pedal loose	Fasten or replace	64–69
	2. Chain dry, dirty or worn	Clean, lubricate, or replace	71
	3. Bottom bracket bearing or pedal bearing out of adjustment	Adjust, lubricate, overhaul	65, 69

Problem or Symptom	Possible Cause	Required Correction	See Page
Chain jumps or skips	1. New chain on worn sprocket	Replace cog or entire freewheel	74–76
	2. Chain worn or slack (non-derailleur bike)	Adjust chain tension or replace	71
	3. Stiff or bent chain link	Replace link or chain . . .	71
Chain drops off chainwheel or cog	1. Derailleur out of adjustment (derailleur bike)	Adjust derailleurs	32
	2. Chain loose or worn (non-derailleur bike)	Adjust or replace chain . . .	71
	3. Chainring bent or loose	Straighten or tighten	67
	4. Incorrect chain line	Correct chain line	73
Irregular pedaling movement	1. Crank, bottom bracket or pedal loose	Adjust or tighten . .	64, 65, 69
	2. Pedal spindle or crank bent	Replace	68, 64
Rubbing noise while pedaling	1. Wrong gear selected	Avoid extreme gears	32
	2. Front derailleur out of adjustment	Adjust front derailleur . . .	37
	3. Front derailleur under angle	Reposition front derailleur . .	37
Derailleur gears do not engage properly	1. Derailleur out of adjustment	Adjust derailleur . . .	32, 37
	2. Derailleur dirty or damaged	Overhaul derailleur	35
	3. Derailleur control lever or cable damaged, corroded or maladjusted	Clean, lubricate, adjust, or replace	39, 40
	4. Chain too short or too long	Correct or replace	71
	5. Cable guides or lever attachment loose	Tighten	39
	6. Front derailleur loose or not straight	Tighten and align	37
Indexed derailleur does not shift properly	1. Cable damaged or corroded	Replace and lubricate . . .	39
	2. Derailleur out of adjustment	Adjust derailleur . . .	32, 37
	3. Chain or cogs worn	Replace	71, 76

Problem or Symptom	Possible Cause	Required Correction	See Page
Hub gearing does not work properly	1. Hub out of adjustment	Adjust hub gear	41–46
	2. Shift lever defective	Clean, lubricate, or replace	45
	3. Control cable pinched or damaged	Free, lubricate, or replace	45
	4. Cable guide loose	Reposition and tighten	45
Rim brake ineffective	1. Brake out of adjustment	Adjust brake	48–53
	2. Brake pads worn	Replace	48
	3. Rim wet, greasy or dirty	Clean rim	29
	4. Steel rim in wet weather	Replace with aluminum rim	86
	5. Brake cable corroded, pinched or damaged	Free, lubricate or replace cable	57
	6. Brake lever loose or damaged	Tighten, free, lubricate, or replace lever	55
	7. Rim seriously out of round	Straighten rim	83
	8. Brake loose or bent	Tighten, free, lubricate, or replace	54
Rim brake jitters	1. Brake loose	Tighten mounting bolt	54
	2. Rim seriously out of round	Straighten rim	83
	3. Rim dirty or greasy	Clean rim	29
	4. Headset loose	Adjust headset	97
Rim brake squeals	1. Brake pads contact rim incorrectly	Adjust or bend ("toe-in")	49, 54
	2. Rim dirty	Clean rim	29
	3. Brake pads worn or dirty	Scrape or replace brake pads	48
	4. Brake arms loose	Tighten pivot bolt	54
Coaster brake ineffective	1. Chain loose	Adjust chain	71
	2. Brake torque arm loose	Attach or tighten	59
	3. Brake hub defective	Overhaul or replace hub	59
Drum brake ineffective	1. Cable or control problems	Free, lubricate, replace	57
	2. Brake torque arm loose	Tighten	55
	3. Brake lining worn or greasy	Reline or exchange brake shoes	61

Problem or Symptom	Possible Cause	Required Correction	See Page
Stirrup brake ineffective	1. Control rod or lever problems	Check, straighten, lubricate, and adjust controls	62
	2. Brake pads worn or rim damaged	Clean, adjust, replace	48, 86
Conventional battery lighting defective	1. Battery exhausted	Replace battery	114
	2. Battery contact defective	Clean, bend, scrape	114
	3. Contact in lamp housing defective	Repair contact	114
	4. Switch defective	Clean contacts, bend spring	114
	5. Bulb loose or defective	Reseat or replace bulb	114
Rechargeable battery lighting defective	1. Battery exhausted	Recharge or replace battery	114
	2. Battery contact defective	Clean, bend, scrape	114
	3. Wiring contact loose	Repair connection	114
	4. Contact in lamp housing defective	Repair contact	114
	5. Switch defective	Clean contacts, bend spring	114
	6. Bulb loose or defective	Reseat or replace bulb	114
Generator lighting defective	1. Dynamo slips off tire	Adjust or bend mountings	115
	2. Bulb loose or defective	Reseat or replace bulb	115
	3. Wiring or contact loose	Repair connection	115
	4. Contact in lamp housing defective	Repair contact	116

FURTHER READING

This short list includes only the most useful and thorough books on bicycle maintenance and repair. Since some of these titles are not generally available at book stores, we have included the publisher's address where appropriate. For additional bicycle-related titles, see the bibliography of any general cycling book or enquire at a library or book shop.

Barnett, John. *Barnett's Manual: Analysis and Procedures for Bicycle Mechanics*. Brattleboro, VT: Vitesse Press (P.O. Box 1886, Brattleboro, VT 05302), 1989.

Berto, Frank J. *Bicycling Magazine's Complete Guide to Upgrading Your Bike*. Emmaus, PA: Rodale Press, 1988.

Brandt, Jobst. *The Bicycle Wheel*. Mountain View, CA: Avocet (P.O. Box 120, Palo Alto, CA 94302), 1992.

Coles, Clarence W., Harold T. Glenn, and John S. Allen. *Glenn's New Complete Bicycle Manual: Selection, Maintenance, Repair*. New York: Crown Publishers, 1989.

Snowling, Steven, and Ken Evans. *Bicycle Mechanics: in workshop and competition*. Huddersfield (U.K.): Springfield Books, 1994.

Sutherland, Howard, John S. Allen, Ed Colaianni, and John P. Hart. *Sutherland's Handbook for Bicycle Mechanics*. Berkeley, CA: Sutherland's Publications (P.O. Box 9061, Berkeley, CA 94709), 1991.

Stevenson, John, and Brant Richards. *Mountain Bikes: Maintenance and Repair*. Bicycle Books, San Francisco, 1994.

Van der Plas, Robert. *The Bicycle Repair Book*. San Francisco: Bicycle Books, 1993.

——. *Bicycle Technology: Understanding, Selecting and Maintaining the Modern Bicycle and its Components*. San Francisco: Bicycle Books, 1991.

——. *Mountain Bike Maintenance: Repairing and Maintaining the Off-Road Bicycle*. San Francisco: Bicycle Books, 1992.

Title	Author	U.S. Price
All Terrain Biking	Jim Zarka	$7.95
The Backroads of Holland	Helen Colijn	$12.95
The Bicycle Fitness Book	Rob van der Plas	$7.95
The Bicycle Repair Book	Rob van der Plas	$9.95
Bicycle Repair Step by Step*	Rob van der Plas	$14.95
Bicycle Technology	Rob van der Plas	$16.95
Bicycle Touring International	Kameel Nasr	$18.95
The Bicycle Touring Manual	Rob van der Plas	$16.95
Bicycling Fuel	Richard Rafoth	$9.95
Champion	Samuel Abt	$12.95
Cycling Europe	Nadine Slavinski	$12.95
Cycling France	Jerry Simpson	$12.95
Cycling Kenya	Kathleen Bennett	$12.95
Cycling the San Francisco Bay Area	Carol O'Hare	$12.95
Cycling the U.S. Parks	Jim Clark	$12.95
The High Performance Heart	Maffetone/Mantell	$9.95
The Mountain Bike Book	Rob van der Plas	$10.95
Mountain Bike Maintenance	Rob van der Plas	$9.95
Mountain Bikes: Maint. & Repair*	Stevenson & Richards	$22.50
Mountain Bike Racing (hardcover)*	Burney & Gould	$22.50
The New Bike Book	Jim Langley	$4.95
Roadside Bicycle Repairs	Rob van der Plas	$4.95

This list is correct at the time of publication. For up-to-date information, write or call for a free copy of Bicycle Books' current full-color catalogue.

Buy our books at your local book shop or bike store.

Book shops can obtain these titles for you from our book trade distributor (National Book Network for the U.S.A.), bike shops directly from us. If you have difficulty obtaining our books elsewhere, we will be pleased to supply them by mail, but we must add $2.50 postage and handling (as well as California Sales Tax if mailed to a California address). For foreign orders, add $3.50 per book for surface mail, or $7.50 for airmail. Prepayment by check or money order drawn on a US bank (or credit card information) must be included with your order.

Bicycle Books, Inc.
PO Box 2038
Mill Valley, CA 94942 (U.S.A.)
Tel.: 1-800-468-8233 or (415) 381-2515
Fax: (415) 381-6912

---

* Books marked thus not available from Bicycle Books in the U.K.